PRAISE FOR
THE VELOCITY MINDSET®

" An extraordinary roadmap for leadership with a fresh, practical, and motivational perspective."

" In *The Velocity Mindset*®, Ron Karr has crafted an easy-to-read, relatable, and instructive guide for those professionals looking to hone their leadership skills. His personal examples coupled with simple tips create 'aha' moments that will serve novice and seasoned professionals alike."

" Ron Karr re-writes the formula for giving you the speed to win big. This book gives you the right stuff!"

" *Velocity* (speed and direction) challenges today's leaders to visualize future outcomes, build vibrant teams, and lead with a calm demeanor. The challenges of leadership are immense, and I recommend Ron's work for any current or aspiring leaders."

" In times of crisis, leaders must quickly cut through the clutter and chaos. *The Velocity Mindset*® will help any leader understand and reframe challenges as opportunities and find success quicker and faster in business and in life."

" *The Velocity Mindset*® helps you ask better questions to quickly get to the big issues—both the challenges and the opportunities. The guiding principles in this book have empowered my leadership team to lead with a velocity mindset that improves sales performance."

BETSY MACK NESPECA, PRESIDENT AND CEO, MACK INDUSTRIES

" Mindset matters, and this book proves that point. More importantly, it gives you the ideas and tools you need as a leader to speed up your growth and reach new destinations. Ron Karr draws from a wealth of personal and professional experience to challenge your thinking and give you new insights."

MARK SANBORN, PRESIDENT, SANBORN & ASSOCIATES, INC.;
AUTHOR, *YOU DON'T NEED A TITLE TO BE A LEADER*

" The velocity mindset is a wonderful fusion of science and business leadership. This book uncovers actionable strategies for guiding what we do every day with a new sense of direction and purpose. In science we know that momentum is the product of mass (what we do) times velocity (speed with direction). Ron brilliantly applies this science to his years of business experience to create guiding principles that will change the way we as leaders think about what we do every day."

STEVE SPANGLER, BESTSELLING AUTHOR; TELEVISION HOST, *DIY SCI*

" Search through all the sales leadership books you want. You won't find science-backed, game-changing strategies like you do inside *The Velocity Mindset*®. Taking Ron Karr's brilliant mindset to heart, I see an entire generation of entry-level sales leaders and managers becoming seasoned in a hurry, the mediocre becoming good, and the good performing at exceptional levels. This is the primer for any aspiring or current sales manager or leader who wants to create legacy and legend during their tenure. This is the book that becomes the sales leader's Bible."

SCOTT G. HALFORD, *WALL STREET JOURNAL* BESTSELLING AUTHOR OF
ACTIVATE YOUR BRAIN; NATIONAL SPEAKERS HALL OF FAME INDUCTEE

"As a CEO and owner of a business, small or large, we have an array of challenges. The coaching and lessons that Ron provided to me and my team elevated our ability to sell and, more importantly, perform better as leaders, all to gain velocity in achieving the next levels of success for the company."

BRIAN TAUBER, CEO, CPP GLOBAL

"This is a very insightful book for leaders, but also a great book for people who aspire to greater self-leadership. Ron's personal and professional success story is living proof that the mindset is stronger than the skill set, or tool-set. This book will give you many chances to arrive at your own personal 'aha' moment that will inspire you to eliminate the barriers to creating the Velocity Mindset® that you need to succeed beyond your wildest dreams. Get a copy for every member of your team. It will be a game changer."

GERHARD GSCHWANDTNER, CEO, SELLINGPOWER.COM

"Through true, emotionally rich stories, Ron Karr reveals how the key to our success is focusing on how we can help other people become successful. C-suite executives, senior managers, and employees in every department of an organization will benefit from this timely book. It will help you become a more effective and mindful leader, no matter what your leadership role is."

BRUCE WEINSTEIN, PHD, THE ETHICS GUY®

"Lots of my friends are authors and ask me to read their manuscripts. The difference with Ron's book is that I loved it and learned so much from every page. You will too. Ron's lifelong experience in helping leaders deal with their seemingly insurmountable problems lays out the perfect roadmap to help you get to where you want to be. Ron's stories, examples, and lessons were all written with a deep and profound understanding of what you need to discover to get what you want. Better yet, when you head out on your journey, you won't be alone. Ron Karr will be right there with you the whole way."

BRUCE TURKEL, AUTHOR, *ALL ABOUT THEM*

THE
VELOCITY
MINDSET®

www.amplifypublishing.com

*The Velocity Mindset®: How Leaders Eliminate Resistance, Gain
Buy-in, and Achieve Better Results—Faster*

For more information, please contact:
Amplify Publishing, an imprint of Mascot Books
620 Herndon Parkway #320
Herndon, VA 20170
info@amplifypublishing.com

Library of Congress Control Number: 2021902552

CPSIA Code: PRFRE0321A
ISBN-13: 978-1-64543-628-7

Printed in Canada

*This book is dedicated to two wonderful people: my mother,
Miriam Karr, and my daughter, Amanda.*

*To my mother, thank you for the mentoring and exposure to your
colleagues who shared so many valuable lessons
they learned from you.*

*To my beautiful daughter, my wish (like that of any parent) is for
you to learn from my mistakes, avoid the pain I lived through, and
live a fulfilling life. This book was written with that intent—for
every reader who invests their time in reading it. Amanda, I am in
awe of how far you have grown as an individual and challenge you
to live each and every day with a Velocity Mindset®.*

THE
VELOCITY
MINDSET®

HOW LEADERS ELIMINATE
RESISTANCE, GAIN BUY-IN, AND
ACHIEVE BETTER RESULTS—FASTER

RON KARR

FOREWORD BY DR. NIDO R. QUBEIN,
PRESIDENT, HIGH POINT UNIVERSITY

ACKNOWLEDGMENTS

THIS BOOK IS A RESULT OF many people's involvement. First and foremost, my editor, John Parsons, did an amazing job in keeping me on track and focused. I have heard many praises on how well the book reads and how easy it is to keep track of the concepts. Thank you, John, for helping make this a bestseller.

To the incomparable Naren Aryal, Kristin Perry, and the whole team at Amplify Publishing, many thanks. When I first pitched the idea to Naren, he shook his head, saying that no one has written an all-in-one leadership and self-help book. But he gleefully cheered me on. When we were all done, his skill and patience helped us prove he was wrong.

To my entire marketing team, what can I say? From Tina LoSasso to Ana Polyakova, John Lusher, Camilla Bignell, and the rest of her colleagues, kudos for helping to get the word out and turning the Velocity Mindset® into a finished piece of work.

To all of my colleagues at the National Speakers Association (NSA), thank you for all your wisdom and the lessons learned over my thirty years of membership. Many of these lessons appear in the book.

And finally, a huge thank you to all my clients who put their trust in me to help them come up with the answers to their problems. The best part of my job as a consultant/speaker is learning about all kinds of industries and meeting so many fascinating people. I have learned something from each of you.

CONTENTS

FOREWORD

RON TELLS THE STORY OF PHIL, the bellhop, so well. In front of an intent crowd, with shoulders slumped and head down, Ron will paint a scene of walking into a hotel after a ten-hour car ride from his home in New Jersey. That's when he meets Phil. Here's what Ron remembers from that meeting long ago:

"Out of the corner of my eye, I see this gleaming smile, sun beaming off the teeth, and it's coming toward me, and I'm thinking, 'Please, don't come near me!' and the next thing I know, he's hovering over me and saying, 'Sir, what's your name?'

"I tell him, 'Karr. K-a-r-r.' And he says, 'You're Mr. Karr? When I heard Mr. Karr was coming, I knew I had to meet this fine gentleman!'"

The audience laughs, and Ron straightens his shoulders and talks about how his weariness evaporated from his long car ride. Then, Ron tells his audience what he wants them to remember: When it comes to your customers, it's never about you. It's always about them.

For more than thirty years, Ron has captivated audiences nationwide with valuable tips about business and life. He's written four books, appeared on TV, spoken to groups as wide-ranging as Morgan Stanley and the NFL, and he's helped organizations on six continents significantly grow their business. He's been a friend to many. He's been a friend to me.

I've known Ron for several decades, and I've long admired his leadership with the National Speakers Association. From 2013 to 2014, he served as president, and in 1997 and 2008, he received the organization's President's Award for excellence.

I've always enjoyed Ron's message. It's full of practical lessons and humorous asides that Ron calls "a New Jersey comeback." Whenever I've heard him speak, Ron shows everyone how to grow their business.

Here, with the book you hold in your hands, Ron will show you how to grow you.

Velocity Mindset®: How Leaders Eliminate Resistance, Gain Buy-In, and Achieve Better Results—Faster is Ron's fourth book. His first since 2009, *Velocity Mindset®* will reveal how you can become a better leader in anything you do.

Ron has a name for what we all need to have—a "velocity mindset." What he means is that we as leaders need to constantly align and realign our thoughts and actions with those around us to achieve a common objective. When we do, we give purpose to our lives and find relevance in everything we do. I so believe that.

When I became president of High Point University in 2005, I began teaching a life-skills seminar to our freshmen class. Like Ron, I use stories to help freshmen understand the concepts of fiscal literacy, leadership, time management, and the importance of ROL.

We all know about ROI—return on investment. It's what we get back from investing our money. I want our freshmen to understand ROL—return on life. That is what we get back from investing in ourselves.

I tell them to find a purpose larger than themselves and invest in it. When they do that, I tell them, they will discover one of the true treasures of life—happiness.

Ron is doing the same thing with *Velocity Mindset*®. In these pages, you'll find the importance of having passion, finding purpose, and understanding what Ron describes as the "art of the PAUSE."

Understanding that art is everything. Leaders need to step back and ask themselves questions. Ron calls it having a "board meeting" with yourself. Then, leaders can figure out how to pivot and help others reach their best results that can affect their lives.

For Ron, that is his definition of success: Ask questions, listen, and step out of your comfort zone to find a new context beyond what you see—and understand—at first. Then you'll learn how to help people be where they want to be, and in return, you'll receive more than you ever knew possible.

Velocity Mindset® is definitely a book for our time. Look around. Change is the one constant we can expect in our world today, and capable leaders are needed now more than ever.

Change unnerves people. For the timid, change is frightening, and for the comfortable, change is threatening. But for the confident, change brings opportunity.

With *Velocity Mindset*®, Ron will help you gain the confidence you need to take advantage of the opportunities you find. Then you'll become more like Phil.

Phil treated everyone he met at the hotel with exuberance, like they were the only person on the planet. When Ron discovered that—"He does that to *everybody*!" he tells his audiences—he asked Phil about his approach. Phil told Ron he wants to help everyone have a "great day." That includes himself.

"Mr. Karr, I've had great days in my life, but I have yet to have the best days of my life."

Velocity Mindset® will help you find your best days. You'll learn how to engage others and create an environment that inspires everyone around you and helps them create the best version of themselves.

When you do, as Ron likes to say, you'll learn how to dance. You'll dance through life because you'll affect others for years to come. What a way to live.

So here's to your first dance lesson. And here's to the rest of your life. God bless you on your journey.

DR. NIDO R. QUBEIN, PRESIDENT OF HIGH POINT UNIVERSITY

A NOTE ON TEXT BREAKS

FOR YEARS, AUTHORS HAVE HAD REASONS to insert a symbol (or an empty line) in the middle of a chapter. These text breaks are used to shift the scene or narrative, to insert a story or anecdote, to supply an explanation, or just to give the reader a rest, a chance to PAUSE . . . and think about what was just said.

For this book on the Velocity Mindset®, we chose our symbol deliberately:

$$- v -$$

The lowercase v is simply the scientific symbol for velocity. The two long dashes are an invention, symbolizing alignment. As you'll see in the book, the concepts of speed with direction (velocity) and alignment are literally a model for successful leadership, in business and in life.

INTRODUCTION

WHEN I BEGAN WRITING A BOOK on leadership, and even before the manuscript was complete, I could not have foreseen my own need to exercise *every* principle contained in these pages. Sure enough, just as I was about to send the final, approved version to my publisher, I received the opportunity of a lifetime.

Since childhood, I have had a heart valve murmur that doctors said would have to be dealt with probably in about ten years' time. However, the unexpected happened. During a routine exam, my cardiologist, Dr. Adam Deutsch, pulled the fire alarm and informed me that my condition was now severe and would require an operation. A noninvasive procedure was out. My best option for a positive outcome was open-heart surgery.

As you can imagine, I was not feeling much like a leader at that moment. I certainly did not feel in charge of my own life. I knew I would need to put everything I believed—the principles you are about to read—to the test.

Then I received an incredible gift. I was already confident in my surgeon, Dr. Erin Iannacone, a woman of impeccable credentials and reputation. But that was not all. From our first consultation, and to my delight, she and her team at NewYork-Presbyterian/Weill Cornell Medical Center proceeded to demonstrate *every single leadership attribute* I had been writing about. She was focused and clearly had the ideal outcome in mind. She actively listened to my many concerns. She was utterly unafraid to have the tough conversations the situation required and, remarkably, did so with an uncommon degree of empathy. Her words, "We will get you through this," were genuine. It was clearly not just a patient-surgeon relationship. It was the beginning of a partnership for life.

True to my surgeon's words and her skill, the surgery went well. With thanks, as I began tackling the recovery process, I was once again reminded of the power and efficacy of true leadership.

— *v* —

Everyone knows what a successful leader looks like. It doesn't matter if they're in sales, a business executive, an entrepreneur, a public figure, or a service provider. It doesn't even matter if they have an official title. Leadership is easy to recognize. Leaders have vision; they have big ideas, and they're not afraid to share them. Their ideas resonate; you wonder why no one ever thought of them before. Their ideas solve a problem—one you can identify with.

Leaders also have a destination in mind, one that others don't see clearly or at all. They know the destination is a better place than they're in now and are eager to make the journey, even when it takes people out of their comfort zone.

Most important, real leaders understand that taking a new path is difficult, not just for themselves, but especially for others. Let's face it; people resist change. They dislike being taken out of their comfort zones. Leaders are not afraid of that resistance. They are not afraid to do what psychologist Scott Peck describes as the painful process of confronting and solving problems.[1]

Successful leaders do not blame failure on others. They always start with themselves and ask what they could do differently. More than that, they also know that *other* people experience pain—especially when *their* desired outcomes are ignored or frustrated. Real leaders will do whatever it takes to solve those problems, even when the process is difficult and frustrating, to make their vision a reality. They will achieve something I call *velocity*.

— *v* —

Can you imagine yourself as that kind of leader? It's easy to recognize successful leadership—*after the fact*. But too often you just don't know how to get there. You tell yourself that leadership is something that only *some* people are born with, that you're just not good enough, that vision and big ideas are just too big to tackle. Worse, you wrap yourself up in a whirlwind of tasks and busyness, hoping for a break but really just trying to resist change and avoid as much discomfort as possible. Sound familiar?

Scott Peck described two kinds of pain. One is the kind that comes with growth, the "necessary nuisance," sometimes severe, that we need to embrace if we want to address problems and reach our goals. That is an unavoidable part of life.[2] But the second kind is worse—what I call the pain of regret. If you spend your time avoiding change, procrastinating, hoping problems will go away, or just trying to forget them, sooner or later you'll find yourself in a worse state. You're faced with the same problems, multiplied, regretting your decisions, and beating yourself up with more self-defeating narratives. Those narratives create drag and resistance, impeding your "flightpath" and robbing you of velocity. Worse, they create resistance in those around you, interfering with *their* velocity and success.

You probably know dozens of people in various stages of resistance—avoiding the "necessary nuisance" required to confront problems and reach a destination. As a result, they are experiencing the pain of regret to some degree. If you're honest, one of those people is you.

This book is a guide for those seeking a better way. Instead of avoiding or moaning about life's problems, I believe you can attain the right mindset for genuine, effective leadership. In the process, you can also accomplish not only your own best outcomes but those of the people around you. This approach, which I have for years applied successfully in the world of sales, is called the Velocity Mindset®.

I'm sure you know the physics principle. Velocity is defined as a "quantity that designates how fast and in what direction a point is moving."[3] This requires both measurable speed and a known direction. When applied to business, velocity also implies that one's direction has an ultimate end or *destination*. It's true, we may need to alter that direction occasionally. As we'll see, it's possible to be going in the *wrong* direction, which will create a whole world of resistance and regret. But the fact remains: we must maintain the *right* direction ultimately to succeed. Speed without direction—as we'll see in chapter 1—is only a formula for burnout.

One more thing. Speed and direction are not the only components of a Velocity Mindset®. The third is *alignment*. Successful leaders don't become so in a vacuum. Their own personal velocity must influence and be influenced by others. As we'll see in part III, a leader's role must include a level of empathy for others' needs and goals, plus the discipline to seek and apply velocity for everyone's benefit.

Now, can you picture yourself as a leader with velocity? It will take a level of fearlessness and toughness you've convinced yourself you don't have. I can assure you that you do. Becoming a great leader is within your grasp.

— *v* —

The principles in this book evolved in part from those in *Lead, Sell, or Get Out of the Way*, my 2009 book for sales professionals. As I spoke about those principles and successfully put them into practice with sales organizations around the country, my vision expanded. It was about more than sales technique. It resonated with CEOs and other business leaders. I knew I was on to something bigger.

Let me share an experience that will make this clearer. In 2013, I found myself on top of a mountain. On a Tuesday afternoon in late July, my mountaintop was cleverly disguised as the grand ballroom at the Philadelphia Marriott Downtown. But I knew better. It was the top of the world.

The occasion was the last day of the National Speakers Association's annual conference. I was the organization's new president. The room was filled with thought leaders, speakers, and authors, many of whom I counted as friends. I stood in the wings, waiting to address over two thousand colleagues. Then I heard the introduction booming across the room, "Ladies and gentlemen, please welcome the fortieth president of the National Speakers Association, CSP Ron Karr." I was overwhelmed. Not for the first time, but in that moment, I felt accepted, loved, and fulfilled. It took me a moment to collect my thoughts.

I felt the support and camaraderie of my colleagues in the audience. But the thought of being in that position would never have occurred to me as a young boy. I told the audience that the moment meant more than they realized.

I explained with a true story. Since childhood, I had struggled with a serious, frustrating condition, one that seemed likely to ruin my life—or so I thought. It was a speech impediment that kept me from pronouncing the letter *r*. Now I can joke about it. "Why would anyone name a disorder using the *one letter* I couldn't pronounce?" I asked the audience. "It's called 'rhotacism' or, as I said it, '*otacism!*' Can you imagine having this disorder and being stuck with the name *Ron Karr?*"

The audience's laughter was mixed with some empathetic wincing. Many could identify with the teenage me, trying to introduce myself to a girl, not able to say my own name, an experience made worse by name-calling and bullying. After the speech—and many other times when I've shared this story—CEOs would come up to say they had had similar experiences.

Clearly, the audience appreciated how far I had come. As a teenager, I didn't think there was a way out. I didn't want to go through the difficult process of change—that is, until I reached a turning point. As an adult, standing with peers who felt the same energy, I knew it had been worth the struggle.

I continued the speech with my plans and vision for the coming year, concluding with an exhortation from my favorite fellow New Jersian, Bruce Springsteen. I challenged the audience, as I have done many times since, to aspire to greater conviction, creativity, and courage. As the music played, they rose to the words of the Boss's inspiring post-9/11 anthem, "Come on up for the rising." It was truly a milestone moment, but there's more to the story.

— *v* —

My rhotacism turning point, speech therapy, wasn't an instant cure—
or an easy one. The embarrassment had become so overwhelming
that I sought out the school's speech therapist—something I had
avoided because I preferred my old comfort zone. But the first forty-
five confusing minutes brought my worst nightmare to reality. It
was impossible. I stormed out in frustration and went back to my
"normal" routine. *I allowed my past experiences to cloud my future.*
But after another year of bullying, I realized something that began
to change my life. *If you don't like the reactions you get in life, you're the*
only one that can do anything about it. You're the only one that can
change the actions that cause those reactions. So I made a choice to
deal with resistance rather than continue the pain of regret.

I found a speech therapist who demanded commitment on my
part. She wasn't kidding. We worked hard for almost two years,
but I could finally say my own name—and lots of other *r* words as
well. (Words I couldn't completely handle I disguised as a New York
accent.) Even though I didn't use the word "velocity" as a teenager,
I had begun to attain it.

— *v* —

Shortly after my mountaintop experience, my life changed in unexpected ways. I'm sure you can relate. My tenure as president limited my speaking opportunities and, in 2014, I had what you might
call a "series of unfortunate events." Thanks to an encounter with a
fast-moving vehicle thirty years prior, I underwent nine surgeries in
two years, mostly for my back. I was unable to travel, so my public
speaking income dropped. I had enough consulting business and was

able to get more, but it was not ideal. I experienced pain, some financial, but mostly physical. But more importantly, I had lost velocity.

Between my third and fourth back surgery, and with hardly any relief, I was introduced to the writings of John Sarno, the famed author, professor, and attending physician at NYU Medical Center. His book[4] described a condition called tension myositis syndrome (TMS) and its underlying causes. He theorized that back pain and other symptoms are an unconscious, self-induced distraction. The physical pain helps us repress deeper, emotional issues.

Another light bulb went off. I knew I had plenty of emotional issues, things that had, without me knowing it, kept me from attaining velocity. Besides my struggles with rhotacism, I also experienced family dysfunction. My father was a Holocaust survivor. He was unable to express the love I knew he had for me and instead resorted to verbal abuse. Over time, I developed a lot of negative, internal stories about my own lack of worthiness. But it was easy to avoid those painful thoughts as I kept busy with my work. Only when I saw how much time had been lost did I begin to realize the real cost of losing velocity.

I told myself that there was no way out of my difficulties. I resisted. Addressing the deeper problem would just be too much to deal with. But time is precious, so I chose the path of change. Despite the time I had lost—or maybe because of it, I took Sarno's advice and began to address my underlying self-esteem issues. It worked. I resolved a ton of issues, especially when I realized how much my father had to struggle with *his* issues. He had not intended me harm, nor did he control my adult life, but I had chosen to interpret his actions in a detrimental way. As I said, it worked. I attained real velocity, physically and financially, *but imagine how much more velocity I could have found if I had addressed these things sooner.*

As human beings, we all tend to repeat our unsuccessful

approaches to problems.* That happens until we finally realize we're not dealing with the *real situation*. I've found this to be true for executives, entrepreneurs, and sales professionals. They are too often dealing with the symptoms, not root causes, as we'll see in this book. My symptom was back pain, immune to muscle relaxers and even surgery. Once I dealt with the root cause, I found myself on a new trajectory, one that brought great gain to myself and those around me.

Think about that for a moment. My velocity was impeded by *my own self-limiting narratives*, things I had buried so deep that it took physical and financial pain to dig them up. I realized I was the only one who could change the actions that were limiting my speed and direction, keeping me from my real objectives. Like overcoming my rhotacism, I knew that real velocity would require a certain mindset, a real commitment, and an application of the principles you'll find in this book.

Isn't that the same thing you face every day? As I write this, many people worldwide are experiencing the financial, social, and even physical trauma of the COVID-19 outbreak. Like so many others, you feel like there's no way out. *You let your past experiences cloud your future.* But it doesn't need to be that way. You can change the actions that result in pain, regret, and loss of velocity—in yourself and in those you influence. You can deal with limiting thoughts, visualize the objectives that matter, and understand the true power and value of empathy. In other words, you can be a leader of your own life. You have the power to control your own destiny, not let it be determined by life events. True leadership means not blaming failure on externals but instead asking how to get around speed bumps and move

---

* Albert Einstein may have said it best: "Insanity: doing the same thing over and over again and expecting different results."

on. Real leaders live with a mantra: "I have the power inside myself to take more control of the results I produce in life."

— v —

This book is divided into three parts, each one part of the toolset for creating a Velocity Mindset®. Each one is grounded in my experience, including the situations I described in *Lead, Sell, or Get Out of the Way* and elsewhere. In some cases, the names have been changed to protect my clients' confidentiality. In others, you'll hear from CEOs and other business leaders who have taken these principles to heart. In all these situations, I have seen remarkable results.

Part I is all about dealing with self-imposed barriers to velocity, including those I encountered often as a young sales professional. In my previous book, I asked what I believe are simple but fundamental questions, "What is your goal or desired outcome? Do your actions support that outcome?" Then, as now, I find that as salespeople, and people in general, we don't ask those questions. If we do, the answers can be negatively impacted by the stories we tell about ourselves, our fear of failure, and the habits of perfectionism and procrastination that keep us from asking those simple questions. The first five chapters will deal with *why* we do these things, and how we can do them differently.

In part II, I cover an important step toward velocity—the power of the PAUSE. Rather than imagining we have all the answers up front (we don't), the secret is to stop and visualize the ideal outcome. We start with a clean piece of paper, literally, and begin to discover the right *destination* that will give us the greatest velocity. (Spoiler alert: the words "destination" and "destiny" are related.) In this section, we'll also explore the hazards of performing tasks versus serving a real purpose and the importance of intuition. Sensing what really matters, to others as well as us, is the key to creating our destiny. Starting the process with the ultimate end in sight is a key factor in attaining velocity.

Finally, in part III, we'll explore the concept of alignment—how we influence and are influenced by others. Achieving the right combination of speed and direction in any business endeavor cannot happen unless others do so as well. This means alignment not only by members of your team but also by those you encounter. It also means finding the right context, identifying the "lens" we use to view our challenges and opportunities.

Alignment requires a quality rarely spoken of in business books: the need for empathy. This is supported by neuroscience, specifically the hormones that accompany social bonding and pleasurable, positive reinforcement. While there is such a thing as too much empathy, it is an absolute requirement if leaders are to succeed in attaining a Velocity Mindset®.

— *v* —

Now, if you're still with me, imagine what it would be like if you had this kind of velocity. It's all easier said than done, I know, especially as we face the challenges of today. With urgent matters claiming your attention, you have less time to pause, reflect, and see things in context. I myself still struggle to overcome personal barriers to velocity, visualize my broader purpose and objectives, and align myself and my actions accordingly. I'm winning the war, and many of the battles, but my own Velocity Mindset® is a work in progress. If you decide to take this journey with me, remember that it's a journey for life. So long as life throws new situations at us, and as our needs and wants change, we must always work on tweaking our Velocity Mindset®. The good news? Doing this will not only avoid creating drag and resistance on our velocity going forward. It will also keep us moving forward toward that "dream of life" we all hope for and help us pass it on.

01

FINDING THE RIGHT MINDSET

01 BECOMING A GREAT LEADER

WHEN YOU HEAR THE WORD *LEADERSHIP,* what's the first thing that pops into your head? Usually, it's about the qualities of a good leader, such as sincere enthusiasm, integrity, good communication skills, managerial competence.[5] These are all good things, but they mainly describe the *how* of leadership—its features, if you will. When it comes to the *what*, the real heart of the matter, real leadership is all about *making other people successful beyond their wildest dreams.*

This definition has fueled my mission as a sales/leadership coach. Sales professionals who genuinely concern themselves with their prospect's success are far more likely to succeed than those who recite features and make the conversation all about themselves. (More on that later.) But this definition goes far beyond sales; it applies to leaders of every kind.

An important distinction should be made here. There is a difference between being a *leader* and being a *manager*,[6] but the terms are often confused. Not everyone who becomes a manager is automatically a leader. By definition, a manager should be adept at using processes of many kinds to direct day-to-day work efforts. Ideally (but not always), they should also have the mindset described in this book.

Now ask yourself a question. What would the world be like if everyone acted like a leader? What would happen if everyone were focused more on others' success? Clearly, I'm talking about a person's *disposition*, not their *position* within a company or organization. Not everyone has the wherewithal to become CEOs, generals, philanthropists, or presidents. There are only so many slots available anyway. But as history and current events prove, the *title* of a leader doesn't automatically make them one. What really matters are their attitudes and especially their actions. With or without a formal title, real leaders have *something inside* that drives their behavior. It drives them to influence those around them.

This brings us back to the question. What if *everyone* was a leader—and acted like it? What would the world look like if more people took responsibility, stopped blaming other people or circumstances, and focused on *their* outcomes? Here are two examples:

When there's not a perfect outcome to something important (and there never is), what would it be like if the first thought were, "What could I have done differently?"

When there's a barrier to *your* success that involves other people (raise your hand if you identify), what would it be like if the first thought were, "I wonder what *their* success would look like?"

Leaders create their own environment for success by getting the most out of the people they lead. This happens not by force but by tapping into individual wants and motivations. A leader knows the strengths and weaknesses of all the players and is driven to help them succeed, no matter the size or composition of the team.

If you've read my previous book, *Lead, Sell, or Get Out of the Way*, these ideas will sound familiar. But *this* book goes beyond being better at sales; it's about becoming a *leader*. Whether you're a CEO, an entrepreneur, a sales executive, a service professional, *or you don't have any leadership title at all*, you can still become a leader. It does involve certain kinds of risk, and a vision and passion for something important, but it is possible. With the right mindset, it's even likely.

— *v* —

To illustrate this idea and get a picture of what leadership looks like, let's go back the early 1980s in Manhattan, the Big Apple. At the time, New York was considered the "murder capital" of the country, so we'll make it daytime—not quite so scary. Say you're at Ninetieth Street. Things look okay, but keep going north. When you get to around 105th, you start to see a lot of run-down buildings, even some empty ones. Not exactly the good old days.

Now picture one of those buildings, six-story, brick, lots of windows; it probably looked great back in the day, but in 1982, not so much. In fact, it's a mess. Like the neighborhood itself, it needs a *lot* of work. Every day, twenty smart people drive by that building and think, "What a waste! I'll bet that could be a great . . ." and they fill in the blank with their favorite idea. Maybe it's an apartment building, offices, shops, or a hotel. But nineteen of those people just *keep walking*.

Ask yourself: what kept them from *doing* something? Let's say all twenty have some practical experience, so it's not just an idle fantasy. It *is* a great building, with real potential, as you can see when you go there today. But they still walked right by and never gave it another thought. They did *nothing* about their big idea. Why is that?

First, it's okay to say there are risks involved. As I said, in the 1980s, neighborhoods like this had real problems. If someone in this group had rehabbed the building, there was no guarantee the neighborhood itself would turn around.

But there's a bigger issue. Every one of those nineteen people thought the idea was just *too big*. So they told themselves stories, things like, "No way. It's a great idea, but it's too much for me. I can't deal with it right now. I'm just one person. I'm not the right person. If I invest, what happens if the neighborhood doesn't come back? Who's got my back? Who do I think I am, anyway?"

In a way, they're right. "Too big" can be risky. But the real barrier was the stories they told themselves. Rather than think about what they *could* do, they focused on the wrong thing.

So the building stays empty. But now, let's go forward from the '80s to today. When that one person out of twenty thought and did something different, an interesting thing happened. That same building was transformed. So were the other buildings in the neighborhood. That twentieth person didn't just imagine a big idea, they took a calculated risk and did something about it.

Instead of listening to the stories in their head, that twentieth person had a different process. They began with a passion for change. Their thoughts went something like this: *"What's my objective here?* What's the first task that supports my objective? What can I do myself, and how much do I need someone's help? If there's a risk (and there always is), who else has a stake in this and can be influenced to share that risk? What's *their* best outcome?" The twentieth person is constantly asking, *"What's the next task, and the one after that?"*

You get the idea. Instead of fixating on why it can't be done or why they're not smart enough or good enough, they focused on what they *could* do. They knew a big idea needs more than a great vision. It needs people (including themselves) who are willing to work through problems creatively, doing the tasks that actually support the objective.

This doesn't mean ignoring the risks, which are a big reason the other nineteen people walked away. They didn't feel that the risk was a valid one, since they didn't have all the answers to what *might* happen. The twentieth person, however, *knew they didn't have all the answers up front*, but that didn't scare them. The risks are real, but so are the solutions and the rewards.

Another important point: leaders know their success is not all about their own efforts. It depends on the efforts of those around them. They don't have to think of or do everything themselves because they surround themselves with smart and capable people. They find the right people to have the right conversations.

If you're telling yourself all this seems obvious, then ask yourself, why did the nineteen others see a great idea but walk away? What made that one person different from the other nineteen? It's not just intelligence and hard work. It's a special quality of great leadership: a mindset combining speed *and* direction—in other words, velocity. It also requires a continuous alignment (and realignment) of their own thoughts and actions, and those of others, to achieve the objective. It's a practice I call the Velocity Mindset®.

— *v* —

Over the years, I've told that story many times in speeches and one-on-one. Everyone can relate, even successful CEOs, entrepreneurs, and other successful leaders. We all have big ideas all the time, but sometimes those ideas are just too big. It's easy to think of reasons why we can't do something big; but it's harder to focus on the things we *can* do. We stay busy with other tasks, but we miss the big opportunities. So I always ask them (and myself at times), "Even though we had velocity in the past, what is it that keeps us from attaining *more* velocity?"

Velocity isn't something that happens easily or overnight. Some people have good natural instincts, but that doesn't automatically make them *great* leaders. Vince Lombardi got it partly right when he said, "Leaders aren't born, they are made. And they are made just like anything else, through hard work." But there's more to it than that. Just embracing hard work is not enough, especially if you focus just on the "whirlwind," those everyday tasks that don't support your purpose. You know the saying: "We're too busy mopping the floor to turn off the faucet." Experience will tell you, hopefully sooner rather than later, that speed without direction is not a formula for leadership. It's just a recipe for burnout.

Here's an example from my consulting practice: a top, high-performing sales rep whom we'll call Bob had been promoted to national account management, but things were not going well. As a sales professional, Bob had been focused on his objective, which was to meet or exceed his quarterly numbers. He was really good at it; his own efforts supported that goal. He'd drop *everything* to fix a problem, please the customer, and close deals at a remarkable rate. But when he was promoted, he didn't automatically transform into a leader.

Bob's objective had changed, but he didn't. He kept his "firefighter" mentality, and his old tasks didn't support the new objective. Whenever a rep had a problem, he jumped in to save the day. His people began to depend on him to close deals and fix their problems. As a result, *they* lost velocity.

A leader's job is not to do other people's jobs. Their job is to make it possible for others to do their jobs well. A leader's success depends on the sum of others' efforts. By playing the hero and fulfilling his ego, Bob relied on his own efforts and simultaneously limited the efforts of others. He had plenty of speed but in the wrong direction. He failed to PAUSE and ask:

What is my job?

How is my objective different than what it was?

What does success mean—not just for me but for those I lead?

A sales manager, *or any other leader*, must identify and assess gaps, coach people in addressing them, and monitor their progress. Imagine how much more velocity his team would have had if Bob had coached them in doing their jobs well, even when he was not there.

A leader's destination is not static; it always changes, so we need to constantly check to make sure of our heading. We need to master the art of the PAUSE, asking if the objective has changed and making sure our actions still support them. As we'll discuss later in the book, this is not always easy.

— *v* —

As a sales and leadership expert, I often saw the results of speed without direction. Many salespeople would spend time and energy reciting everything they know about a product's features without once considering that the prospect had a challenge or a problem that they didn't see. They didn't figure out how to position their offering in a powerful way for the client, so they missed sales opportunities and alienated prospects who might have become long-term partners.

In *Lead, Sell, or Get Out of the Way*, I dubbed this practice "puking." The acronym PUKE stands for "People who Utter Knowledge about Everything." It stems from the false assumption that a salesperson's primary role is to educate their prospects before—and sometimes instead of—showing any concern for their actual needs. This probably sounds familiar, but here's a test. If you were in the process of procuring something important, ask yourself how thrilled you'd be to hear:

Option One: A sales rep who's ready to give you ten reasons why their product is the best, even though eight of those reasons have nothing to do with you. (Cue the crickets.)

Option Two: A sales rep who did everything they could to understand your situation and make sure you made the right decision. In the past hour or so, I'm sure you've probably blocked calls or ignored emails from someone practicing option one. But when someone practices option two, that's an example of velocity. That person is acting like a leader.

Let me share an example. Early in my career, I was a sales rep for Royal Business Machines, and sold copiers to businesses in New Jersey. Frankly, I was seduced by their new technology, a dry toner system that produced great quality copies without all the mess and bother of manually refilling the liquid toner. (Only dry cleaners loved this.) The technology was revolutionary. It grabbed customers' attention—and mine—but the machine itself was limited in other ways. Whenever one of those missing features came up, I was told that the copier would have it—someday.

The problem was we were competing with the likes of Xerox. Their big machines could do *everything*. They were Goliath, and we were trying to be David. In companies throughout my territory, one of their machines on a single floor could serve the copying needs of *everyone* on every floor.

At first, we attacked the problem the traditional way. In our pitches, we listed all our copier's features and promised new ones that were on the way. We "puked" all over the place, showing off *everything* we knew. We also did some fancy, razzle-dazzle talking to fill in the gaps. You can probably guess our success rate. We had plenty of speed but no direction. We thought we had all the answers up front. We didn't stop to ask about the prospect's objectives or show curiosity or empathy for their challenges. So, in the end, all we had to offer was a better price—and even that was not enough to save the deal. Why? Because we were having the wrong conversation. We were having a *sales* conversation instead of a *leadership* conversation.

But that all changed one day.

I had been trying to sell to a company in New Jersey without success. Like a lot of other sales professionals, I thought, "If only I had something new to sell, then everyone will buy it." It was all about features—or, to be honest, future features. I had positioned myself as a copier salesperson, which instantly invited comparison to the big Xerox machine on the third floor. When that happened, and I couldn't offer the same features, I was out on my butt, which happened too many times.

So, one day, I PAUSED. I had a "board meeting" with me and myself. Like most people, I could have blamed the company for not having a copier feature that seemed important to *me*. But instead, *I asked what I could do differently*. I didn't like the reaction of getting kicked out, but I knew I could only change my own actions. So I asked myself the question, "What are you really selling here?" Then I realized, *I'm not selling a copier; I'm selling a communications vehicle.* I should be selling *outcomes*, not products.

This changed everything. The next time I walked in the door, I wasn't going to talk about my machine. Instead, I decided to have a different conversation—with different positioning. I started by asking the office manager if he agreed that copiers were nothing more than communications vehicles for the company. He did, and his whole demeanor changed. Then I asked what his three biggest challenges were when it came to their current communications vehicle.

Suddenly, he became animated and emotional. His biggest issue was time. Their machine was great, but staff members had to go to the third floor, even if they only had to make one copy. They might stop and chat along the way. They might have to stand in line. It might take up to two hours! When I asked what the total time was, the answer was shocking: the equivalent of two full-time employees! So I asked, "How would you like to get those full-time employees back?"

He said the magic word, "How?" I answered that I wasn't competing with their big machine. I wanted to fill a gap—something that was frustrating their progress. My machine was perfect for doing those single copies, reducing two-hour tasks to five minutes. I suggested putting one on every floor—reclaiming those two full-time employees.

I started selling multiple machines—three at a time.

My fortunes changed because I took responsibility. I didn't blame my company for not having a feature. When I didn't like the reaction, I asked what action *I* could do differently. I changed the conversation and created a new context, to reveal gaps I didn't know they had. I did not know the answer up front, so I asked, and I really listened. I didn't have the word for it at the time, but I had *velocity*.

— *v* —

So the key is not only to identify *your* objective but also to know the objectives of *others*. What are the objectives and career goals of everyone on your team? Knowing the objectives of others is no easy task, as we'll discover later in the book, but it is essential. They will change, so we have to keep paying attention. When that happens, we must pursue the actions supporting the goals of those you want to lead. In doing so, you'll support your own objectives and satisfy your own purpose for being here. In other words, you'll be a leader.

There's an important aspect of human behavior to mention here. When it comes to productivity, there are two different ways to do any job: meeting an immediate *need* versus satisfying a longer term *want* or desire. As most managers are painfully aware, it's all too common for people to do the minimum, just what they need to do to keep their job. Less often, people do whatever it takes to exceed expectations. They want something fervently enough to go the extra mile, and then some. As we'll see, true leaders know how to make this distinction, in those they lead as well as in themselves.

Let's face it; we're all human. If we're not paying attention, we become trapped in speed without direction. We focus only on what we *need* to do instead of what we *want* to do. In our preoccupation with an idea or goal, we imagine we know all the answers up front, even when we clearly don't. Instead of pausing, asking questions, and really listening, we fill our time with a long list of actions that don't support any real objective.

There are plenty of barriers to achieving velocity, as the next chapter will discuss. Even technology designed to make our lives more efficient can add to our list of tasks without letting us see—or address—the real purpose. Think about all the times you checked your email rather than do something "important, but not urgent," or scheduled a meeting for the sake of having a meeting, or checked out a new CRM feature—just because it felt better than tackling a big idea. We do all these things because it seems easier than admitting we don't have all the answers.

Lack of velocity is tragic for two reasons. One is simply burnout. Performing tasks devoid of purpose eventually takes a toll on our emotional and physical well-being. Without the meaning and satisfaction of reaching the right goal, we eventually lose heart, taking it out on those around us or indulging in self-destructive behavior.

The other consequence is even worse. Without velocity, when we're hyperfocused on tasks without purpose, we're less likely to respond to a big idea—like that building on 105th Street. We are more susceptible to limiting thoughts, negative stories we repeat about ourselves, which we'll explore in the next chapter. We're more likely to succumb to fear of failure, to perfectionism, and to procrastination. Instead of imagining creative ways to address an issue, we find reasons to say, "It's too much. Who do I think I am, anyway?"

Both results deprive us of our passion—that sense of purpose and meaning that makes us want to get up each day and savor the results at day's end. When our actions lack purpose, the results are disappointing, and we lose any passion we may have had. No matter what the challenge is, it's hard to take risks about something you're not passionate about. Think of the difference between the teacher in *Ferris Bueller's Day Off* ("Anyone? Anyone?") and that one inspiring teacher most of us can remember—the one who saw meaning and purpose in their work.

For me this was the late Don Kreitz, my high school history teacher and the school's football coach. When he taught with great passion, you were riveted as he brought historical characters to life. As for setting an example, he would walk between buildings in winter in his short sleeves. When I asked why he wasn't freezing, his response taught me something about mind over matter. "If you don't mind," he said, "it doesn't matter." It's all about the story we tell ourselves. You get to choose which version of the story you want to live by. He chose the version that demonstrated his passion and focus, and you cannot have velocity without passion.

Finally, remember that *we do not have all the answers up front*. If we think we do, then we are not shooting high enough. Success goes to those who ask questions and listen to find new contexts, not to those who stay in their comfort zones.

Having a Velocity Mindset® can mean dealing with habits extending as far back as your first job, your first relationship, or even your childhood. It requires fearlessness and a willingness to embrace the things we *can* do rather than the reasons why we can't even try. It will also require that you PAUSE, frequently, to ask what your objective really is and whether your actions support that objective. As later chapters will explore, it also requires a capacity for empathy and connection to align yourself and those around you to the tasks that support your mutual vision.

It's not an easy road, but it is the road to genuine leadership that will yield a tremendous return on your investment of time, money, and effort.

02 DEALING WITH LIMITING THOUGHTS

IN THE FIRST CHAPTER, I ASKED the question, What would the world be like if everyone, regardless of title or position, acted like a leader? If your answer was positive, then the next big question is, *Why don't we do it more often?* What prevents us from adopting a mindset that makes leadership a normal everyday practice?

The answer is the negative stories we tell ourselves.

Part of being human, maybe the most important part, is that we tell each other stories. Sometimes, they are simple communication— just the facts. You know. "I remember there's good hunting over that hill," or "Watch out for saber-toothed tigers!" We also add motives and plot points, starting with "Once upon a time," to fill in the gaps with ideas and possibilities, real or imagined.

We can also "go big," connecting our stories to greater ones. We recall (and add to) the legends, myths, and archetypes that define us. We tell stories around campfires, paint them on walls, shout them in the street, whisper them to friends, and stream them on Netflix or Zoom. No other species relies as much as we do on our ability to put thoughts into words.

But we don't just tell stories to other people; the audience is often ourselves. This is also a perfectly normal part of being human that psychologists call an internal monologue or self-talk. They are part of our planning and problem-solving process. The stories we tell ourselves are based, more or less, on things that actually happened or conversations from the past, liberally mixed with our imagination. Sometimes, our internal stories are true, and at other times, not so much. But no matter what, the stories we tell ourselves are a part of us.

Sometimes, these stories are positive. They energize us and give us confidence and creativity as we plan the tasks that support our objectives. But sometimes, the opposite is true. Even in the most outwardly successful, charismatic, gifted people, you'll find their inner voice is saying otherwise. In a 2016 NPR interview, actor Tom Hanks admitted his struggle with negative self-talk. "No matter what we've done," he said, "there comes a point where you think, 'How did I get here? When are they going to discover that I am, in fact, a fraud and take everything away from me?'" In fact, many truly gifted individuals—leaders in their fields—admit to these thoughts, sometimes known as the "imposter syndrome." But somehow, they managed to succeed—and lead—when they otherwise might have failed. Despite their internal, negative voices, which never disappeared, they found velocity.

Overcoming these limiting thoughts is not easy or automatic, especially when we're engaged in tasks without purpose. When we're not focused on outcomes, when we're stressed or stuck in survival mode, the internal stories of "I'm not good enough" come in, loud and clear.

Let's go back to chapter 1 for a minute. When I was selling copiers by "puking" a list of features, I was kicked out at least fifty times and hadn't closed a sale in over four months. I was discouraged, broke, and depressed. My frequent companions were thoughts— voices created from my past—saying, "You're not a real salesperson. Who do you think you are? You'll never amount to . . ." You get the idea. I couldn't control the reactions I was getting from prospects, and I certainly couldn't stop the unhelpful voices that were a constant drag and resistance in my soul. I could have stayed there, but I decided there was something I *could* control: my own actions. When the pain was sufficient for me to do that, I found a way to deal with my negative self-talk.

The secret is not to eliminate those thoughts by sheer force of will. You can't, and neither could I. The secret is to recognize these limiting thoughts or stories for what they are when they occur and ask the real questions, "What's the *outcome* I want, and what can I actually *do* here?"

— *v* —

One afternoon, I was an interested spectator at my daughter's summer league softball game. The team had managed a respectable season record, qualifying for the playoffs. Unfortunately, their opponent that day was a team that had demolished them during the season. Their star pitcher had a devastating sixty-five-mile-per-hour fastball. At forty-three feet from home plate, her pitching was equivalent to major league heat. In a regular season game, she had pitched a blowout against my daughter's team. It was so ugly that the game was called in the third inning. You might say their mood was not good.

As I watched her team sitting and waiting on the bleachers, eyeing the other team, their mindset was clearly along these lines: "There's no way we can get a bat on that ball," I imagined. "It's hot and muggy. What's the point? We should just call it and go have pizza." But the coach knew me and what I did for a living. Right before the game started, he looked up and, to my daughter's chagrin, hollered, "Hey, you! Mister Motivational Speaker, you got five minutes. Motivate them!"

If you've ever had teenage kids—or been one yourself—you know how easy it is to motivate and inspire them—*not*! I had given hundreds of speeches, but I was never quite as nervous as I was for this one. As I made my way down, studiously avoiding "the look," from one particular team member, I had plenty of limiting thoughts myself, but I knew theirs were worse.

I started with a classic motivational question, "If I ask you *not* to think about pink elephants, what are you thinking about?" They all answered, "pink elephants." The mind can't process the negative, I told them. If they were telling themselves, "I hope I don't strike out," then they weren't thinking about "*don't*" or "*not*;" they were thinking about striking out—a self-fulling prophecy. Every thought and action was in relation to striking out. To change from focusing on their limiting thoughts, they had to go to the desired *outcome*. I asked what the thing was they wanted to do at the plate, and they answered, "Get a hit." So I asked them to promise only one thing—that when they were at bat, all they would visualize is where the hit ball would go.

They won the game.

It wasn't my doing; all I did was give them an option. Instead of entertaining a limiting thought ("Don't strike out!"), each girl chose instead to consider an action that supported their objective ("Get a hit!").

Happy endings are not guaranteed. But the story illustrates a point I have seen repeatedly played out, by CEOs, sales professionals, entrepreneurs, and would-be leaders of every kind. We all have internal narratives playing in our heads—all the time. Many of them are negative and limiting. The problem is, *we can't focus on more than one thing at a time*. Contrary to popular belief, humans are not multitasking by nature. Neuroscience research has found, conclusively, that the brain does not do things simultaneously.[7] At best, we switch rapidly from one thing to another. When we switch back and forth frequently, it gets rough. We lose time and efficiency and make more mistakes. It saps our energy.[8]

So when we have limiting thoughts, the rest of us follows along. We succumb to the idea, "I'm just not good enough" or "I don't deserve to win" or "Who do I think I am?" And, lo and behold, our actions follow suit. Even when our qualifications say otherwise or we objectively know those narratives are untrue, our limiting thoughts have the microphone, so to speak. They are like the drag and resistance that causes a plane to lose velocity.

But, as my daughter's team proved that day, as have many others, it doesn't have to stay that way. We can deal with our limiting thoughts.

— *v* —

The first step to dealing with limiting thoughts is recognizing where they come from. In my own case, it didn't take a genius to figure out that I had issues with self-esteem, coinciding with my rhotacism and my history with a loving but flawed family. My self-talk was an echo of my father's frequent criticism, which was repeated and amplified (by me) with familiar gems like, "What is wrong with you?" and "You'll never be a . . ." and so on. But eventually I recognized where those thoughts were coming from and, more importantly, how to deal with them.

Here's the tricky part. Without those criticisms and challenges driving me, I would probably never have acquired the skills to be a good salesperson, executive coach, and public speaker. Adversity built up certain qualities, for which I'm grateful. But because I embraced those thoughts as an unconscious narrative, I missed out on even greater accomplishments. By leaving issues unresolved, as we'll explore in chapter 4, I deprived myself of the opportunity to gain more velocity sooner.

My situation is not unique. Everyone has life experiences that drive perceptions of who we are, what we can or cannot do, and what we have the right to do. Many times, these are negative, even when they're unintended. A casual, negative remark by a teacher or other adult in the midst of a child's fanciful creativity may begin a self-narrative of not being "good enough." It may also provoke defiance and determination to overcome, whether or not the talent exists. (Caution is required here. Giving false praise is *not* the alternative to criticism, whether to a child or an adult. People are remarkably good at BS detection, even at a young age. Insincere praise can create as many limiting thoughts as does cruelty or criticism.)

Fortunately, when dealing with my own limiting thoughts, I discovered a way to address the velocity-limiting habits we deploy as defense mechanisms, like procrastination and focusing on tasks without purpose.

— *v* —

In the fall of 2019, I enrolled in an intensive coaching program with Sophie McLean, a renowned wisdom teacher and author of the book

The Elegance of Simplicity.[9] It consisted of five tough sessions. In the last one, she hit me over the head with a game-changing distinction. "Whatever your father did to you," she said, "he did for his own reasons, *one* of which was a feeling of love." We agreed on that part. She continued, *"Whatever someone does or says to you,* you *are the one who interpreted what it means! It's not the other person doing it."* Wow!

Think about this. I was dealing with my perception of what his actions and words meant. It was *my* story. When I realized that, I suddenly gained more power in not letting those stories I made up control my life.

Interpreting others' words and actions—creating a story—was what held me back. I had created my own limiting thoughts. So I accepted responsibility for my *perception* of myself (my stories, good and bad), which was not the same as the *reality* of who I was, what my objectives were, and what actions would support those objectives.

Once I knew that about myself, I also knew that others had the same problem and that I was onto something. In fact, it has taken my coaching of senior executives to a whole new level of success. *Having a self-focused mindset is the number one barrier to velocity.* Knowing and focusing on the success of others, who all have their own limiting thoughts, is the key to your own velocity.

— *v* —

Recognizing and taking responsibility for our limiting thoughts is only the first step in the process. Old habits die hard; they have an energy of their own that is hard to overcome. To make matters worse, our brains don't handle more than one thing at a time, so an engrained, negative narrative can become, by default, the only voice in the room. Our resulting actions by default therefore become tasks without purpose. For sales professionals, that means "puking" up features instead of actively listening for unmet objectives. For CEOs, it means flooding one's colleagues with statements, missions, and projects that don't consider a customer's unmet needs. For anyone with leadership aspirations, it can mean countless tasks based on a self-focused mindset. In every case, our own limiting thoughts are inevitably behind these fruitless endeavors.

So, as I said earlier, the second step is not to eliminate limiting thoughts by brute force of will. Instead, it is an exercise I call "the art of the PAUSE."

Since we can't focus on two different things at once, we have to give ourselves the opportunity to think differently. Whenever there's a drag or resistance to some desired outcome, the trick is not to push harder. As mentioned earlier, that is merely speed without direction—the recipe for burnout. Instead, the answer is to PAUSE and ask:

One: What's the story I'm telling myself here? Am I letting some past narrative or assumption tell me what I can or cannot do? Is it affecting me or those around me? I can't control what other people do (or did), but I *can* control what I think about it and what I can do about it.

Two: Am I seeing all the *objectives*—not only mine but also those of everyone else? I won't be able to meet every single need, but I should at least know what they are. Maybe they'll reveal something new.

Three: What is my job? I can't do other people's work for them, but I can at least identify the gaps and help them achieve their objectives. (This also means knowing when to admit that an objective can't be met.)

Obviously, there are times to do this and times to wait—let's say, *after* a contentious meeting has ended. Until your team members are adept in Velocity Mindset® practices, it may be wise to sort out these questions on your own.

In business coaching parlance, this process is also known as *being present*. It involves actual listening (not just hearing the words), reflecting or mirroring back what others have said, and giving undivided attention or focus, as we'll cover in later chapters.

A good leader will already have an instinctive grasp of this process, as his team members will attest. Phrases like "he's a great listener," "she really gets us," and "they know how to inspire" are symptoms of business velocity but not the root cause. The real key is the leader's ability to pause, take responsibility, and maintain a mindset that is outward-focused, not self-focused.

Everyone has limiting thoughts. But whatever their cause, such thoughts do not have to limit our speed and direction. Even if they have become habits, limiting thoughts can be replaced. No matter what you think about things of the past and how they have created drag and resistance, it is possible to overcome them and achieve a Velocity Mindset®.

03 THE PSYCHOLOGY OF INFLUENCE

BEFORE MOVING ON TO THE TECHNIQUES for achieving velocity, it's important to understand some of the neuroscience involved. Our bodies have evolved specific mechanisms that control how we react to stimulus. Scientists have discovered a number of chemical compounds—hormones—that play important roles in maintaining the human body. They also have effects on our moods and behaviors.[10]

This chapter is a layman's overview of three such hormones: cortisol, oxytocin, and dopamine. It's based on scientific consensus but is not a scholarly treatment of the subject. These hormones are complicated, and their roles are constantly being examined. However, one thing is clear. Whether we are influencing others or the other way around, our physical systems have a lot to say about how we feel and what we are likely to do.

The object of this chapter is not to give you a foolproof scheme for manipulating others artificially with hormones. Besides the ethical and moral problems that raises, there is simply no way to create measurable lab results in a business environment.* However, it is useful and beneficial to know that certain practices produce higher levels of certain hormones which, in combination with other factors, are more likely to result in bad or good results.

In a sense, we are "experimenting" with other people's responses. But the goal here is to change *our behavior*. If we understand how our words and actions affect other people physiologically, then we'll have more reasons to gain velocity.

— v —

Cortisol: the Stress Hormone. Produced by your adrenal glands, cortisol has many functions. It controls blood sugar levels in the body, as well as inflammation, memory formation, salt and water balance, and blood pressure.[11] Normally, cortisol levels are higher in the morning, when we wake up, and decrease throughout the day. But one of its more fascinating aspects is how cortisol is involved in our response to stress.

Whenever we encounter a stressful situation, such as imminent danger, increased cortisol acts like an emergency alert system. It stimulates the liver to produce more blood sugar and helps the body convert fats, proteins, and carbohydrates into usable energy— preparing the body for a potential fight-or-flight response.[12] It also suppresses other systems that might interfere with our response to danger. This was one reason our distant ancestors survived attacks

---

* Manipulating human *behavior* is not new, of course. Casinos are infamous for creating conditions and responses, many of them hormonally based, that induce people to gamble more. Advertisers in general employ similar tactics to capture attention and manipulate emotional behavior. However, few business situations have sufficient control of their physical environment to control hormonal reactions—even if it were ethical to do so.

by predators and other dangers. And, thanks to the rules of natural selection and survival of the fittest, they passed this cortisol "alert system" down to us.

Today, we still face life-threatening situations, such as assaults, collapsing buildings, or vehicle collisions, that trigger cortisol responses and that same burst of energy. But we also experience other, less life-threatening situations that trigger the same response. Thanks to this, our bodies react by creating cortisol, treating stressful situations, more or less, like an oncoming predator. So when a salesperson interrupts your day with an unwanted barrage of information, or a manager calls you on the carpet for something that bugs *him*, your cortisol level goes up. You're ready to fight or fly, so to speak, but not much else.

At normal, relatively low levels, cortisol promotes a sense of normalcy and *engagement*, but when cortisol is elevated, it heightens our sense of readiness for action and *resistance*. The cause of stress may be a truly dangerous situation but is likely not. However, the body doesn't really know the difference. We are on alert, hormonally speaking, and are less likely to process things that don't relate to the stress we feel. Only when our brains send the all-clear signal will we feel open to new information and those who bring it.

— *v* —

The relationship between stimulus and our cortisol levels was brought into focus for me by interactions with my colleague and fellow public speaker, Scott Halford. His excellent book[13] on the human brain provides helpful insights on *why* we tend to respond to stressful (cortisol-producing) or rewarding (oxytocin- and dopamine-producing) situations in similar ways—and what we can do about it.

As leaders, if we aspire to influence others, our responsibility is to make sure the *mental* environment is conducive to conversation. That means having an awareness of cortisol reactions and finding ways of communicating that don't trigger them. In that way, we actively take responsibility for the outcome.

It does not always happen that way. On a scale of one to ten, Halford described a common response to sales situations we experience regularly:

When you interrupt someone, the stressor hormone cortisol is going to pop up no matter who you are. When you interrupt someone, and you're a salesperson, you will likely see even more of a stress response, probably a level six. So, meeting the prospect/ customer where they are and understanding that your first job is to edge that cortisol down to your four-to-five level on your chart is the first goal.

The nuance is that cortisol at lower levels, but still visibly present, is where focus and interest lie. The one-to-two level is mild interest. Four-to-five is keen, focused interest. Six-to-seven is anxious interest and broken focus, and eight-to-ten is discomfort with the only focus being to get away.

So, a little bit of cortisol is necessary for interest. There is some excitement when the adrenalin part that travels with cortisol gets involved at the four-to-five level. That's what you get when you have norepinephrine (a form of adrenalin in the brain) and cortisol—very energized interest and focus.

When you bond with the prospect/customer by making your visit about *them*, and it feels to them like what you're talking about could be true and a benefit to them, they begin to feel connected to you because it feels like you "get them." That's where oxytocin is introduced and over time and with consistent results from the salesperson's recommendations, the oxytocin and bonding become even stronger. That's when they refer the salesperson to everyone they know. That's when . . . dopamine is at play. Dopamine pairs with oxytocin to make a happy, bonding connection . . . one that is difficult to beat.[14]

— *v* —

Oxytocin: the Trust and Connection Hormone. The so-called "love hormone," oxytocin, is a neurotransmitter, a chemical that acts like a signaling mechanism in the hundred billion or so neurons in your body. It's produced in the part of your brain called the hypothala-mus—the part that regulates automatic functions like body tem-perature, hunger, and sleep. Oxytocin also plays a significant role in social bonding and social recognition, as well as sexual drives that are outside the scope of this book.

Like cortisol, our oxytocin levels change when we receive outside stimulus. It could be a gesture or a word from someone close by, a signal of friendliness or interest seen as positive or supportive, that increases oxytocin production. We *feel* a sense of closeness or con-nection, often accompanied by a pleasurable sensation from higher levels of dopamine. When those feelings prove to be accurate, we tend to trust the person more and act accordingly.

Our distant ancestors developed this response when it came to successful procreation (that's the sex part), but also when it came to connecting with fellow tribe members. Oxytocin responses nudged them to more prosocial behavior, more cooperation and trust. It would certainly influence better success in hunting and gathering efforts. Later, it probably eased the way for that unique, human activity: trade and innovation. Over the millennia, tribes that cooperated more tended to live better lives and reproduce more successfully. And so, *voilà*, their oxytocin-fueled habits passed down to us.

Now, let's consider oxytocin responses today. Interrupting a prospect with a list of irrelevant facts or confronting a colleague with a list of grievances would likely trigger a rise in cortisol, as mentioned above. But what would happen if instead you communicated genuine interest and support? The most likely response would be elevated levels of oxytocin, nudging the prospect or coworker to greater openness, more sociability, and feelings of connection. They would be more likely to listen and engage; they feel their interests and yours are more aligned.

We need to be careful here. Obviously, if you act or speak in a way that elevates someone's oxytocin levels, but then *betray* that sense of trust, then you'll create a cortisol-laden reaction that's worse than not even trying. If you signal your interest in someone's success, you'd better mean it. Also, this is *not* an endorsement of oxytocin sprays or other artificial means of influencing behavior. Besides being ethical minefields, these techniques are also scientifically suspect.[15]

As we'll explore later in the chapter, the role of oxytocin is significant in any situation where you are proposing a new idea and seeking agreement. It holds true for all leadership situations, whether you're selling a product, starting a business, or building your company's long-term strategy.

— *v* —

Dopamine: the Pleasure Hormone. Intricately connected with oxytocin is another neurotransmitter hormone called dopamine. Known as the "feel-good" hormone, it is created in the brain *and* in the adrenal glands. Dopamine is our built-in reward system for activities like sex, eating food we crave, or other actions that satisfy our needs. Besides the pleasure reward, dopamine boosts our mood, motivation, and attention, as well as regulating our movement, learning and emotional responses.[16] One study involving the use of Ritalin in treating ADHD[17] found that the drug increased the amount of available dopamine, improving mental performance by helping the brain decide whether a goal is worth the effort. Dopamine increased the sense of reward, leading to more willingness to take on difficult tasks.

But like all hormonal responses, our dopamine reactions are not always ideal. In fact, they can be destructive. When we artificially trigger these chemical rewards—let's say, with drugs, alcohol, or the thrill of taking risks like gambling—our bodies are telling us we've satisfied a need when we've really only created an illusion. This isn't a sermon about addiction, but it does have an application to having a Velocity Mindset®.

Recently, in the wake of the economic chaos around the Great Recession of 2008, I received calls from two different sales organizations. Both wanted to hire me as a keynote speaker, but I wanted to be sure that I was a good fit. One executive said that his salespeople were depressed. Sales were down across the board, and they really needed someone who could lift their spirits. He wanted someone who could "entertain the troops," tell jokes, and in general make them feel good and take their mind off their troubles. The other executive had the same problem. Sales were down and his people were unhappy about it. But he wanted someone who could find new ways to meet their objectives. The keynote had to be a satisfying, motivating group experience, not just a pleasant diversion.

I said no to the entertainment gig and yes to the other. I am *not* saying the first company was wrong to want a good time. In fact, I recommended someone who delivered that kind of performance. But my approach, although it involves jokes, has a different objective. It's true that when I speak publicly, I incorporate humor because it opens up the audience to hearing new concepts; they are less guarded. (In professional speaking, we also have a saying: If you want to get paid, you'd better make them laugh.) But my role in using humor is not to be a humorist. It is used to trigger an audience's sense of connection (oxytocin) and pleasure (dopamine) as I introduce new concepts, ideas they can use to increase their level of success. The goal is not just the good feelings; it is to encourage velocity.

— *v* —

These three hormones are constantly at work as we attempt to lead others. If we can read the signs when others are experiencing stress (cortisol), greater connection (oxytocin), and a sense of satisfaction or reward (dopamine), then it will help guide our interactions and make us better leaders.

To illustrate this, I developed a role-playing exercise based on one of my interactions as a sales consultant. First, I set the scene:

A while back, I was working with a financial services company whose clients were largely retirees and conservative investors. Their approach to acquiring new clients was to cold call prospects in their homes, usually in the afternoon. From past experience, they knew it took an average of five calls to sign up a new investor. So they asked me to accompany one of their advisors on a call to see if there was any way to reduce the total number of calls.

The financial advisor, a four-year veteran, was under the impression that he had to build a social relationship first. Otherwise, no one would buy from him. So, on a call with a polite, middle-aged couple, he spent the first *twelve minutes* talking about the pictures on their wall, including their kids, and other small talk. Clearly, he was interrupting their day. I could tell the couple was wondering why he was even there but were too polite to say anything.

To the audience, and to my role-playing volunteers, I briefly describe the cortisol response, using Scott Halford's one-to-ten scale.

Cortisol Levels

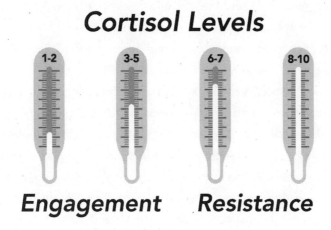

1-2   **3-5**   **6-7**   **8-10**

Engagement   Resistance

I explain that below three, there is little engagement. They may not have a wall up, but you don't really have their attention. At around four or five is the area of increased engagement, where the hearer is listening attentively and ready to go. At six or seven, the walls start to go up. They wonder why you're there, tell themselves they already have an investment person, think about other things, and are not really listening. By the time it gets to eight-to-ten, the person has checked out. They're ready to run, so to speak.

As leaders, if we want to influence anyone about any idea, we must first take responsibility for the environment. In sales, when we're calling on someone who's not expecting us, *we are an interruption*. If you've ever been interrupted in the middle of your day, just ask yourself, "What's my cortisol level?"

So I take two volunteers from the audience and run them through the same scenario, with one playing the part of selling financial services. I ask the person playing the prospect to guess their own cortisol level just *before* the meeting started and *after* the first few seconds of the actual meeting. They typically answer, "one or two" before the meeting and "six or seven" after. Why does the person playing the prospect change the numbers to a much higher level of cortisol, to seven or higher, after only a few seconds of the meeting? Because the person playing the salesperson does what most salespeople do. They bore their prospects with descriptions of their products and services without any context. Back to the role-play on stage. I ask the prospect where they would put their cortisol level after those first few seconds of listening to the salesperson. The answer is usually six or seven. "They're boring me with features I'm not interested in. I've got other things to do. And besides, I already have a financial advisor."

At this point, I take the salesperson aside and privately tell them to try a different approach. Cut the chit-chat down to a minute and then get the prospect to open up about what their real *wants* are. The conversation should be, "I know you have an advisor, and I'm not here to talk about stocks and bonds. I'm here about your future. Do you mind if I ask you a question?" After getting an assent, the question should be (as it was when I was with my original client), "When it comes to your future, what are three things you *want* your money to provide for you?"

Immediately, I saw the role-playing prospect's eyes go up as they mentioned things like kid's tuition, travel, and comfort in retirement. Something was different, so I asked where they put their cortisol level, which was, "four or five." They were engaged. I asked them to repeat the second role-play for the audience, so they could see the response. Explaining their emotions, the person playing the customer said, "My guard went down because it was about me and my plans. I didn't feel like I was being sold something." And here's the kicker. The prospect did 90 percent of the talking! They felt the salesperson was there for them. When you talk too much in a moment of influence, you actually have less power than you think.

After the role-play, I went on to describe the other two hormones. Oxytocin is associated with trust and connection, but trust has to be earned. By asking what was important to the prospect, rather than pressing a self-focused narrative, my role-players were showing how that trust could begin to be built. Similarly, most people begin to have positive feelings (dopamine) once that trust and connection began to be established. When I asked, the prospect said they felt better when the conversation was about things that were important to them.

I have repeated this experiment many times in my leadership and sales keynotes, with large audiences and one-on-one. Every time, people's emotional response changes. When the conversation moves from self-focus to customer-focused, feelings of resistance and resentment fall, while feelings of engagement, trust, and enjoyment rise. And your velocity takes off because you now have speed with direction!

By the way, do you remember the financial services company who hired me to work with their leadership team on this concept? You may be asking what the results were. They reduced their sales cycle of closing a new investor from five calls to three. Imagine how much velocity this organization gained in growing its market share. This same process, based on an awareness of brain chemistry, works with anyone you are trying to influence. This holds true whether that person is a customer, an employee, a colleague, or someone in your personal life.

— *v* —

Finally, throughout the book, I will refer to the phenomenon of *burnout*, which psychologists attribute to (among other things) not being in control of how a job is carried out or being asked to complete tasks in conflict with one's sense of self.[18] Those who have suffered from burnout can have abnormally low levels of cortisol,[19] making it difficult to engage with tasks and other people.

Burnout is also the result of having speed but no clear direction—or even the wrong direction—both in one's personal life and in a business leadership role.

The condition has different symptoms. A 1991 study of US teachers[20] defined three *types* of burnout that hold true for individuals in most professions today:

Worn Out—where a person gives up because of too much stress, too little reward, or both.

Frenetic—where a person keeps working harder and harder, trying to resolve a stressful situation and/or seek a suitable reward for their work.

Underchallenged—where a person has low stress levels, but their work is unrewarding.

Regardless of the symptoms, burnout is a sure sign that people are not focused on the right tasks that have purpose or meaning. In the ensuing chapters, we will discuss many facets of this problem and how to realign ourselves to attain true velocity.

In a sense, our bodies are wired to respond in predictable ways. Whether it's coping with stress (cortisol), achieving connection (oxytocin), or reinforcing satisfying outcomes (dopamine), we are psychologically capable of benefiting ourselves *and* those around us. If we can read the signs and act accordingly, we will see the difference and achieve greater velocity.

04 FAILURE AS A MEANS OF SUCCESS

IN CHAPTER 2, WE TALKED ABOUT limiting thoughts, stories we tell ourselves that, consciously or not, prevent us from attaining velocity. One of the biggest self-limiting stories in our heads is our *fear of failure*. Another limiting narrative, ironically, is our *fear of success*. It is possible to have both of these narratives holding us back.[21] Even leaders are not immune, although their leadership qualities are defined by how well they deal with these fears.

But all this begs the question: What is failure?

In professional baseball, the player with a career batting average of .300 will likely end up in the Hall of Fame.[22] Pause for a minute to think about that. Someone who has failed to hit the ball seven times out of ten throughout their career is considered an outstanding success. The reason is that they learn from those mistakes knowing their successes carry rewards. When a .300 hitter is in a slump, they do something about it. They look at films, work with a coach, identify the flaw, and do something different their next time at bat. Successful leaders follow the same pattern. They do not let failures stop them; they take steps to learn from them and avoid making the same mistakes. Failures, handled properly, are only speed bumps on the path to rewards.

So why does failure so often put us off our game, so to speak? Why are we so ready to believe a narrative about "*being* a failure" instead of just having failed—and learned something from it? Let's look at it objectively. Success and failure are just ordinary, measurable parts of everyday existence. Right? Take these examples:

You either hit the ball or you don't.

You either make your quarterly sales quota, or you fall short.

Your team either meets its project goals, or it doesn't.

Either the board approves your team's plan, or they say, "not this year," (which can be code for "no way" or "go away.")

It's called life in the real world. Take the four examples I just listed. The consequences of failure are real. A strikeout, a drop in revenue, or a business setback are not imaginary problems. But how we view failure has everything to do with our minds and the self-limiting stories we tell ourselves. They can include shame and embarrassment, our sense of self-worth, uncertainty, and many other self-narratives,[23] stories that are more to do with feelings than with facts.

If we're not paying attention, we let our *fear* of failure (and/or success) become bigger and more powerful than the failure itself. This seems obvious when we say it out loud, but very often our fear of failure just sneaks up on us. We let our cortisol-fueled responses call the shots. Our fear of failure can even result in actual *physical pain* as well as *habits and behavior* that limit our potential velocity.

— *v* —

To show you how powerful the fear of failure is, I'll share a story of my own. Ever since an encounter with a fast-moving vehicle over thirty years ago, I have had back issues. The pain was significant, so I sought the advice of several doctors and surgeons, who all said the same thing. "I have seen patients with worse scans than yours who are *not* incapacitated, but I've also seen patients with better scans who are worse off than you." My choice was to have a number of vertebrae immobilized, or "fused," by inserting and attaching titanium rods on either side of the spine. The fused areas, formerly moving independently, would now act as one. The only question was how many levels of the spine should be fused.*

I had an excellent surgeon, Dr. Andrew Sama, who successfully performed four surgeries on my spine. Initially, he proposed fusing only three levels, then going further later on, if necessary. This was sound advice. However, as we often do, I also sought a second opinion. That doctor recommended a more aggressive approach— fusing six levels immediately rather than waiting. Both alternatives were medically sound, so I had a choice to make.

From the start, I was afraid I would lose more mobility after the surgery. So I was inclined to agree with a more cautious approach. My own fear of failure paralyzed me (pun intended) from taking the more aggressive approach suggested by the second opinion. Eventually, the problem was successfully resolved when the four surgeries fused *nine* levels of my spine. But my fear, *not the doctors'*, prolonged the problem. In hindsight, had I overcome my fear of a more aggressive approach, I would have reduced my time of disability by at least

---

* If you're curious, there's a diagram at https://en.wikipedia.org/wiki/Vertebral_column. To give you an idea of the severity of my situation, Tiger Woods had had only one level fused, and he found it difficult to resume playing. Eventually, I had *nine* levels fused, from the pelvic bone to T-10.

six months, with fewer surgeries! My fear had prevented me from gaining velocity sooner.

During this saga, the second-opinion doctor asked a simple but profound question. When I expressed my concern that an aggressive approach would make me more restricted, he asked, "How much flexibility do you have *right now*?" Even though my answer was, "I can't move," I was reluctant to follow his advice. I settled for the gradual approach.

My fear of losing more mobility prevented me from really listening to his question and taking more aggressive action. In hindsight, if I had listened, I could have reduced the number of surgeries and returned to normal activity much sooner. Neither recommendation was medically wrong, but *I was responding to the wrong question*.

Today, even with some restriction, I have more movement and no pain when I swing the golf club. I'll have to admit that Tiger Woods is still the better golfer, but I'm back in the game. This is all thanks to Dr. Sama and his amazing team at New York's Hospital for Special Surgery.

But the biggest lesson came from the matter-of-fact question, "What's your situation *right now*?" Had I listened then; I'd be further ahead now.

But back to the story. After one of my surgeries, I was laid up for months. I was slowly recovering mobility, but the pain was still there. My body had failed me. In my mind, the outcomes my doctors had discussed about relieving my pain and getting me back to normal had also failed.

This was an unfair assessment on my part, but the fact was that I was frustrated by the pain, by the fear of pain, and by an ongoing sense of failure. I was doing some consulting but was not able to resume my usual public speaking roles. My story, at least the one I told myself, seemed like one of personal failure.

Fortunately, it was then that I was introduced to a book[24] by NYU professor John Sarno, a doctor of pain medicine and author whose work has revolutionized thinking about pain and its underlying emotional causes. His work not only helped me overcome the literal pain, but it also helped me understand how to move from fear of failure to seeing failure as an opportunity for success.

— *v* —

Sarno was curious why people experienced back pain when their nerves were dead. He wondered how a dead nerve could even generate pain in the first place! Through years of research, he concluded that the pain was a condition he termed tension myositis syndrome or TMS, our ability to *create* pain as an unconscious, self-induced *distraction*. The pain of TMS, he said, was there to help repress deeper, more painful emotional issues.

I began to realize that TMS explained a great deal when it came to pain in the body. Think about one of the most common medical complaints of the 1980s—ulcers—which are hardly mentioned at all these days. Today, that pain has been replaced by others, like back pain and fibromyalgia.

Let me be clear. Such ailments are real and can have diagnosed, physical causes. However, it's also true that the mind, out of our fears, insecurities, and frustrations, can distract us from deeper problems by creating actual, physical pain. Very often people stop having that kind of pain only when they addressed the underlying problem, the thing that was actually *causing* the pain. Sarno described the various pain symptoms of TMS as camouflage. "As long as the person's attention remains focused on the pain syndrome," he said, "there is no danger that the emotions will be revealed."[25]

In his subsequent book, *The Mindbody Prescription*,[26] Sarno also described personality traits and behaviors common to those experiencing TMS. These piqued my interest. In the course of my consulting, I had often observed this type of velocity-draining behavior in other professionals, whether or not they were experiencing (or talking about) any physical pain. I wondered, if there were ways to address *these* behaviors and their underlying limiting thoughts, then it would not only alleviate the pain of TMS but also lead to greater velocity.

One of these personality traits is a familiar one: perfectionism. Sarno described it as coming from "a deep need to demonstrate to ourselves and to the world that we are truly worth something."[27] In my role as a consultant, I often saw it as the result of overemphasizing the "failure-is-not-an-option" mantra. Perfectionists are generally ambitious, hard-driving, and self-critical. They describe themselves as highly responsible, conscientious, concerned, and prone to worrying. So far, these traits are typical of many in leadership positions, but there's a catch. Such people unconsciously set standards for themselves that are literally impossible to meet. So when they inevitably fail to meet such a standard, they experience even more unconscious shame and rage. The "lather-rinse-repeat" cycle continues, and they become even more incapable of velocity. Rather than viewing failure as an opportunity for change, they fear it, perpetuating their own self-fulfilling prophecy.

The other trait Sarno describes is less well-known: goodism. These are people who put the needs and desires of others before their own, unconsciously trying to prove their own worth. They are driven to be helpful, even to the extent of sacrificing their own needs. It's a trait not limited to rank-and-file team members. Those in management positions who constantly try to be the "good cop" or the "buddy" tend to do so because of the pressure to be "good enough." In doing so, they set themselves up for more failure—and the cycle continues.

— *v* —

Armed with these insights, I began to address a number of personal issues, as described earlier in the book. As I went through every phase of my life, I realized that the physical ailments that happened during those phases were related to emotions hidden in the subconscious. My cortisol levels were probably sky-high, making the problems even worse. But thankfully, I experienced relief from the physical back pain as I began to come to terms with my past.

I began to realize how much further I could have gone—how much more velocity gained—had I not been dealing with those mind-induced ailments. But something even more profound emerged. Had I realized all this in my twenties, I merely would have been angry at myself. But now, having made the journey, I had learned something from my failures—something far more valuable to my clients.

I learned the secret of moving from fear of failure to seeing failure as an opportunity for success. *The secret is in learning to ask—and answer—the right questions.* This is the path to finding a true Velocity Mindset®.

Think about the major league batter at the beginning of this chapter. Had he focused on fear of failure and the consequences of being released or sent down to the minors, he would have been focusing on the wrong question, "What if I miss?" Maybe his inner narrative would have produced physical pain, perfectionism, or both. In either case, that fear of failure would have had a self-fulfilling result: a loss of velocity. But instead, he asked a different question, "What can I do differently?" The result is still seven failures out of ten or, in other words, a .300 batting average and a path to the Hall of Fame.

Or recall another version of the same story with my daughter's softball team. Fear of failure ("What if I miss?") was replaced by opportunity ("Where do I hit the ball?"). A Velocity Mindset® starts with asking the right questions.

— *v* —

To achieve actual success, we must learn how to overcome both our fear of failure *and* our fear of success. If you think these two fears are unrelated, just recall the "imposter syndrome" example in chapter 2. Hugely successful people can feel they are unworthy of recognition they have clearly earned. They may associate the excitement of success with feelings of anxiety.[28] They are plagued with doubts about their ability to deliver results or with worries about the changes success might bring.[29] In any case, when these fears arise, we need to PAUSE and take the time to ask what failure and success really mean.

Without giving away the rest of the book, here are some invaluable tools for addressing these kinds of fears:

Do not let the fear become a reality. The more we entertain our fears without questioning them, the more real they become.

Do not merely avoid fear, surrender to panic, or get mad about it. When that surge of doubt and "What if?" thoughts comes crashing in, PAUSE and actually complete the conversation. For example, if you calmly pose the question, "What's the worst that could happen?"

and the answer is reasonable, you follow up with, "So, then what happens?" Keep that up for as long as you need to. Soon, the fear of failure (and/or success) will be replaced with creative, constructive steps for pursuing actual success.

As you keep answering these questions, your fears will subside. This will allow you to become more creative in identifying the steps needed to move forward.

Always keep in mind that velocity is not a static condition. In our lifetimes, we will never fully "arrive" at perfection. We are not perfect; we make mistakes, like the seven out of ten failed at-bats of a .300 average Hall of Famer. The only way to attain that velocity, and overcome our fears, is to learn from our mistakes by asking the right questions.

— *v* —

This was all brought home to me by my friend and colleague, innovation guru, author,[30] and Speaker Hall of Fame Stephen Shapiro. He described a problem at a major airport. Passengers were constantly complaining about the amount of time they had to wait for their baggage. The airport's reputation and revenue were at risk, so clearly they had to find a solution.

Management's fear of failure (losing business) was a major factor. It had narrowed their focus and probably increased cortisol levels all around. However, their first instinct, speeding up baggage processing, was a nonstarter. The added costs would far outweigh the benefit in shorter wait times.

Fortunately, they learned to ask a different question. "The key to speed and innovation is to avoid immediately focusing on solutions," Shapiro said, "but rather to step back and ask better questions." Instead of asking how to speed up delivering the bags, they asked how they could reduce wait time—a completely different question addressing the very same issue. Brilliant! In the end, the airport slowed down the passengers by moving the baggage carrousel. Doing this increased the distance they walked, thus reducing the time they waited at baggage claim.

This event also highlights another issue we'll cover later in the book. Those who labor under a fear of failure are prone to being *self-focused*—as opposed to being focused on the needs of their customers, team members, or other constituents. Self-focus leads to a host of velocity-defeating behaviors, including engaging in tasks without purpose and a rinse-and-repeat cycle of failure and more fear. Only by asking different questions can we focus outside ourselves and our fears and begin to move with speed *and* direction.

— v —

In my own practice, this principle of failure—and what to do about it—has come up repeatedly. I'm often called in to coach clients on the hiring of new team members—not just people with good CVs but those with real leadership potential. I tell the clients they have to "go deep" when conducting interviews. Everyone they interview will be wearing a mask, so to speak, because they just want the job. Many are afraid to fail, so if my client were to say, "We want someone who is proactive," they're likely to get a glib answer, "Well, I'm so proactive, my last company didn't know what to do with me!"

Wrong question; meaningless answer.

Instead, I counsel my clients to dig and discover how a candidate makes decisions. First, I advise them to probe the candidate for specific actions they consider as being proactive—what they did, how they did it, and the results. Not everyone can answer that, but if they can, the next step is to seek out *contradictory evidence*. This means asking them about a time when they weren't proactive but should have been. Ask what they did or didn't do, the results, and what they would do differently next time.

The important thing is not whether people fail—as we all do. The important thing is to find out if they learned. As they relate how and why they failed, and especially how they might have done things differently, candidates with real leadership potential will establish that essential skill: the ability to build from previous mistakes on their way to becoming that .300 hitter.

— *v* —

Finally, there is one more example of how the fear of failure can impede velocity, but how viewing failure correctly (by asking the right questions) can do the opposite. Many executives are in the habit of interviewing employees, from line operators to floor managers and everyone in between, in an attempt to root out inefficiency and perhaps discover the "bad apples" in their operation. It's a natural impulse for those who want to increase efficiency and get everyone to "buy in" to their vision. Unfortunately, if they ask the wrong questions, the results can be disastrous, making velocity impossible.

Picture this. If the executive team is narrowly self-focused rather than seeking broader outcomes—with objectives that elicit *everyone's* passion—then their questions will not be well received. The interviewee may well be afraid of failure, real or imagined, and thus will have a defensive, narrow focus. Their cortisol levels will probably be elevated, and their answers will be self-preserving at best. The resulting data will be skewed by their fear of failure and possible retribution. Those who respond will be plagued by thoughts of perfectionism ("It has to be *exactly* right or I'm really in trouble!") or goodism ("I'll show them how capable I am, that I'm worthy!") or both. Neither response will increase velocity.

Fortunately, there are proven ways to create a culture of safety, not fear, which is key to the definition of velocity. One of these is the Lean production process for maximizing customer value while minimizing waste.[31] While a full description of Lean is outside the scope of this book, it is worth noting its coaching-based improvement practices that actively foster a velocity mindset.

One of the key steps of Lean is to interview those involved in the manufacturing process. This is known as the "Gemba walk," from the Japanese word *genba*, meaning "the actual place." It involves regularly going to see the actual process, understanding the work, and asking questions.[32] Properly implemented, the Lean process results in actionable data and the reinvention of a more efficient process. It involves the use of scientific method as the foundation for improvement (not failure, but experimentation to learn), and the daily practice, or *kata*, of improvement techniques. Lean practices ensure that, inside that safe environment, the right questions inspire creativity and a mutual desire for velocity from all involved. When the sparkle of discovery replaces the stigma of failure, a passion for learning and improving fuels both urgent and durable change.

To put it in velocity terms, rather than probing for what is inefficient (which is interpreted as "Why are *you* not efficient?"), executives must *ask the right questions*, to elicit input on the objectives that are important to *them* and how *they* would make something better or more efficient. You get the idea. The wrong, self-focused questions lead to a CYA conversation, squelching any creative thought. The right questions inspire creativity and a mutual desire for velocity. Even when failure is involved, as it often is, the questions must always focus on ways to learn from failure and enlist the interests of everyone involved.

— v —

When I was in management in the computer industry way back when, I was asked what I valued in a team member. I replied (as I would now) that I valued someone who was willing to try new things, make mistakes, but then pick themselves up and try something different. I did not appreciate someone who always stayed under the radar, unwilling to try anything, only doing what it took to get by.

Through my coaching with CEOs, I have found that some, though regrettably not all, have learned how to handle failure well. They have learned to manage the results, not the process. They value the initiative of those who took chances and were not afraid to fail but learned from those mistakes when they did.

By definition, failure is not intrinsically a good thing. It has real consequences. Deliberately seeking ways to fail is not a viable strategy for anything, much less good leadership. But failure, recognized promptly and rationally, always represents a basis for change, provided we learn from and build upon that experience.

On the other hand, fear of failure, that cortisol-fueled self-narrative of doubt and insecurity, is only a recipe for prolonged pain (including the physical kind) and velocity-killing behavior. But with the right questions focused outside ourselves and by visualizing what we *can* accomplish, failure is simply a record of our path toward a goal.

According to folklore, when asked about his numerous early failures to perfect the electric light bulb, Thomas Edison once quipped, "I have not failed. I've just found ten thousand ways that won't work."

05 THE LAW OF FOCUS

FINDING A VELOCITY MINDSET® CAN BE a challenging process. We have to deal with our own limiting thoughts, including the potentially paralyzing fear of failure. We also must acknowledge and deal with our own brain chemistry, which can narrow our responses and derail our progress toward an objective—if we let it. The way to overcome these impediments to velocity, and find the mindset required of a good leader, is what I call the Law of Focus.

By this, I do not mean using sheer willpower to keep yourself and everyone else moving along a particular path. That's the *speed* part of velocity, which, as mentioned earlier, is only a recipe for burnout. A Velocity Mindset® involves both speed *and* direction, as well as the alignment of everyone in relationship to a clear, shared objective. That objective must be compelling enough to inspire our passion.

— *v* —

A while back, I was the first keynote speaker at a CenterBuild conference sponsored by the International Council of Shopping Centers. At the event were over five hundred mall owners, real estate tycoons, and construction company executives—veterans of some of the most complicated development projects in the country.

I addressed the crowd, gathered for lunch in a tent outside the Phoenix Biltmore Hotel, and ask them a challenging question. "Why is it that you depend on each other, each one responsible for different parts of a mall project, and each of you are late, and make each other late . . ." There were plenty of nods and smiles. "Then how is it that, even with all the lateness, come hell or high water, the mall opens on the advertised date?" The reason, I explained, is the Law of Focus.

Everyone involved in such a giant construction project is focused, collectively, on that *one thing*, that date on the calendar. It's amazing what things can be worked around and dealt with, I told the audience, when that kind of shared focus and passion is present. It generates an *intensity* in looking at each situation, analyzing it from all angles, and coming up with creative new ideas. If we don't focus on what we want, it will never become a reality. It requires a shared passion to drive you forward even when things aren't going the way you want.

After the speech, I asked the event planner how she thought it went. She commented that people at these lunches were usually leaving by dessert time, to play golf, but that everyone had stayed.

— *v* —

Needless to say, since then, my emphasis on the Law of Focus has become an integral part of my coaching CEOs and other leaders. Without a doubt, focus on a single, compelling, and shared objective is the single most important step in acquiring the right mindset for successful leadership. In practice, however, there are several formidable barriers to taking this step and sticking with it.

The first barrier may seem obvious. If there is no clear objective, then there can be no focus. Period. But finding such an objective is tricky. It must be connected to actual, tangible *results*, not emotion. For my CenterBuild audience, meeting the final completion deadline meant *everything* to their financial and reputational success, completely separate from their personal feelings.

Other key aspects of such an objective are its size and its strength. To qualify, the objective must be *big enough* to satisfy the interests of everyone involved and *strong enough* to keep them from straying off course. For a giant construction project, an immoveable opening day fit both requirements. Every owner, planner, contractor, subcontractor, supplier, and service provider had different, interlocking business goals, but the "master deadline" loomed over everything. It also had the gravitational pull, as it were, to drag everyone back to reality during moments of chaos and confusion.

Discovering such an objective requires several characteristics discussed later in the book. One of these is the ability to visualize outcomes using a "clean piece of paper," without pretending to know all the answers up front. Another is the ability to actually *listen* to others, with actual empathy, rather than just hearing their words. This includes not only allied businesses, such as the companies engaged in a massive construction project, but also people within your own orbit. If the objective is not big enough to interest them or strong enough to compel their attention, then it is not the clear objective you need.

When considering the importance of having a clear objective, also remember that having *too many objectives* is a sure way to derail focus. As mentioned in chapter 2, it is literally impossible for humans to process two things at once. If we try, by switching rapidly from one task to another, then both objectives will suffer. This emerges frequently in my consulting and coaching practice. When a client has been struggling with the same issues for a while, I question whether both are just as important. If one is clearly the main objective, then I suggest they focus on that and stop getting distracted.

— *v* —

Another barrier to the Law of Focus is inflexibility. The old Yiddish proverb "Man plans, and God laughs" is there to remind us that even our best ideas can and often do run afoul of reality. Circumstances will inevitably change, undermining past assumptions and forcing us to recalibrate, reset, and restart. (If you really need an example, just consider the COVID-19 pandemic and its disruption of every business on the planet.) By remaining inflexible in the face of change, we render our original objective insufficient as a point of true focus.

The solution, of course, lies in our ability to *pivot*. This well-worn business term is not limited to desperation—our response to catastrophic or disruptive changes. Setting a new "plan B" objective can come from simply seeing no results from trying, and retrying, the original strategy. Pivoting can also be the result of seeing new growth opportunities for the first time.[33]

Our ability to pivot, personally as individual leaders and collectively as the companies we lead, depends on the same qualities that helped us form compelling objectives in the first place. By visualizing desirable outcomes without pretending to know all the answers up front, we are more likely to come up with sound alternatives and contingencies. These will, in turn, form the basis for new or modified objectives. By genuinely listening to others, we are less likely to be surprised and more likely to regain velocity quickly. In other words, the Law of Focus, properly followed, will help us plan for the unexpected.

Being prepared to pivot requires us to be passionate about our original objective but to also be ready with alternatives in mind when unforeseen problems arise. It also requires that we be sensitive to real-time data to make sure those alternatives are still valid. Perhaps most important of all, we need to be willing to move swiftly and not be paralyzed when things change. Often, the worst decision is to do nothing.

Years ago, as a volunteer EMT, I experienced this kind of "focused pivot" firsthand. Our clear objective, hammered in through rigorous training, was to always maintain calm and stabilize the victim in whatever situation we encountered. Medical expertise came second.

But on one call, a cardiac event, I happened to be the first on scene and dashed full speed into the residence. My cortisol level was probably sky-high, and I ran right past the victim, who had been having a heart attack while sitting quietly by the door that I just barged through! I immediately knew I had failed to calm anyone. I had probably freaked out the victim and lost his trust. However, I was prepared to pivot. Knowing the objective was to maintain calm, I immediately handed the situation over to the next EMT, who successfully handled the situation.

I was focused on the objective (maintaining calm) and therefore able to recognize the unforeseen problem (me) and pivot to an action that supported that outcome.

— *v* —

The Law of Focus can be derailed by another behavior detailed later in the book: the self-focused mindset, as opposed to an outcome-focused mindset. If we keep focusing on what we need emotionally and not on the total outcome that both we and others need, then we will lose their support.

A self-focused mindset happens quite naturally when we view everything through our own "lens," fueled by self-narratives and fears discussed earlier in this section. In sales situations, it takes the form of focusing on features. In executive management, it takes the form of tasks without purpose. In every situation, it encourages us to hunker down and avoid any risks.

An outcome-focused mindset is entirely different. Whenever I work with a new executive team, I walk them through an exercise called Strategic Intent. Simply defined, this means their shared vision of the success they're after. (This will be discussed in more detail in the next chapter, "Start with a Clean Piece of Paper.") The power of this exercise is twofold. One is coming up with their primary outcome or objective, but more important is the bonding achieved in building that outcome together.

By following this exercise, if everyone is involved in defining it, they are more likely to follow it. Once you have a clear outcome that everyone can *buy into*, building subsequent plans is easy, because that shared intent serves as a "true north." It helps everyone ask the right focused questions and find the right solutions.

Notice that I said, "buy into," not come to full, unqualified agreement. In group situations, everyone needs to voice their opinions, and universal agreement is hard to achieve. But once we have buy-in on the best outcomes, forward motion is likely. It is the buy-in we must have in order to gain velocity.

— *v* —

As we will see, there is great power in a clear, shared objective, one that elicits the passion and harnesses the collective efforts of every member. Without such an objective, we will not be able to persist in the face of unforeseen events or pivot when that course is warranted. With it, we will overcome our own negative stories, handle our peculiar brain chemistries, and shift our fear of failure into viewing failure as potential growth and opportunity.

In other words, we will discover our Velocity Mindset®.

02

CREATING

OUR

DESTINY

06 START WITH A CLEAN PIECE OF PAPER

Once the basics of creating a Velocity Mindset® are well understood, the next phase is actually *doing* something about it. No amount of clarity about limiting thoughts, brain chemistry, or our fears of failure or success will accomplish anything unless we apply these to actual tasks. Of course, these must be *meaningful* tasks, as we'll discuss in chapter 8.

Your role as a leader is to enable others to achieve a desired goal. So it begs the question: What is that goal? What is the objective, the ideal outcome that inspires passion in every member of the group? What is the outcome that is unique to you, the one that others have not yet imagined? To put it in physics terms, velocity is defined as speed with direction. So to determine the right direction we must identify the right *destination*, a word with the same Latin origin as *destiny*.

This is a serious matter. The ideal outcome always seems obvious—*after* you have clearly defined it—but is often unclear in the moment. The problem is *we allow our past experience to limit our thinking*. We confuse short-term, necessary steps, like making more money, with the long-term outcome.

Once we know the outcome everyone has a passion for, it will lead to actions that support it. It will drive everyone to accomplish those actions and pull them back into alignment, like a giant magnet, when unforeseen obstacles arise. But until we define that outcome, we are prone to making the same mistakes, failing to learn from them, and failing to attain velocity.

The secret to defining that singular, compelling destination is the process of visualization, or what I call *starting with a clean piece of paper*. In fact, when working with clients, I mean that phrase literally.

— *v* —

In the early 1990s, I worked closely with a chemical manufacturer connected with the copper mining industry. Over a twenty-year period, they had developed (at great cost) and patented a chemical reagent that reduced the cost of mining copper by a whopping 50 percent! With this one product, they had single-handedly rescued the US copper mining industry from bankruptcy.

But their glory was short-lived. As is common in such industries, competitors reverse-engineered similar but somewhat inferior reagents and began offering them to mining companies for next to nothing. Increasingly, the mines began demanding competitive bids, reducing everything to a downward-spiraling price war. When the largest copper mining company in the United States started the bidding process for a three-year deal, I was asked to consult with the chemical company's senior management. My job was to help them prepare for a meeting with the mine's sourcing group.

My first question was, "What do you want as the result of my intervention?" Their answer was, simply, "We want to win the bid." But they were answering a different question—not the one I asked. They were answering based on what they knew, based on constraints of the past and what they thought the future could be. I said, "What I'm asking is for you to start with a clean piece of paper. You can create this relationship, this deal, the way *you* want it to be, irrespective of what happened in the past—or what you think can't happen."

As has happened many times since then, their demeanor changed, and their passions began to emerge. Cortisol levels probably dropped, and oxytocin levels increased. They began to imagine a different reality as their passions started to come out. "Why do we have to bid?" one said. "We started this industry; we saved it!" After some questioning, they said they wanted a negotiated agreement for ten years (the life of the patent), not a bid for a three-year contract. They also declared they wanted a 75 percent share of the market, not their current 25 percent. They wanted an agreement on the basis of value, not on price.

We'll continue this story in the next chapter, describing *how* the company put this idea into practice. (Spoiler alert: They succeeded beyond their wildest dreams.) But for now, it's important to see *how* they discovered their ideal outcome. Rather than dwell on past experience—allowing it to define their actions—they PAUSED and gave themselves permission to visualize the thing they were passionate about. By literally starting with a clean piece of paper, writing down what they wanted the future to look like, and sharing it, they found the right destination.

— *v* —

To visualize the ideal outcome, you must regularly remove yourself from a whirlwind of distractions. These include tasks that are urgent but not important, as will be discussed in chapter 8, the limiting thoughts, and any preconceptions based on past experience. Doing this does not require a mystical, "mountaintop" experience. However, it does require practicing what I call the art of the PAUSE. It starts with one fundamental question:

> If you could create your ideal destiny, from scratch, without any regard for what you believe is possible, and not based on past experiences, what would it look like?

I know this is an audacious question, to say the least. But it's an important one for three reasons:

- It brings out your passion, which is critical for ensuring success.
- It eliminates perceived restraints that may have held you back in the past.
- It gives you something to rally around—something that is fundamentally and personally meaningful.

When responding to this question—preferably on a clean piece of paper—be sure that your answers are *specific* and measurable. Also keep in mind: *making more money is not a valid objective*.

The question may be applied to many situations. As a sales account strategy, it would be phrased as, "What is the ideal relationship you want to have with this client or prospect?" When hiring a new team member, it would be, "What does success look like for *this* person?" When embarking on any new venture, it would be, "What does success look like for me, for my team, and for those whose needs we're serving?"

Sometimes, this exercise can be done in your head, hopefully as a routine habit. At other times, it must be done explicitly, with a clean piece of paper and with others participating. In either case, the object is to stop past experience from interfering with your clear view of the outcome. With practice, that outcome will become an indelible destination on your map to greater velocity.

Visualization of this kind is actually supported by neuroscience. This was pointed out by Psychiatrist Srini Pillay, following the 2008–2009 financial collapse.[34] He noted that we stimulate the same brain regions when we visualize an action and when we actually perform that same action. He said this process holds true whether the visualized action is a new business idea, the process of recovery from physical trauma, or enhancement of an athletic activity. Remember the story of my daughter's softball team? When they visualized the desired outcome (getting a hit), it was not guaranteed but certainly more likely.

The same principle also applied to my recovery from back surgery, as I related in chapter 4. I had allowed my past experience (and my fears) to limit my thinking. But as I envisioned my best outcome—to be free from pain, to enjoy an active life, and to better serve my clients—I began to find better, more creative ways to identify and deal with velocity-limiting behaviors like perfectionism and goodism.

— *v* —

The outcome from your clean sheet of paper cannot be trivial or solely for one person's benefit. It must have significance for everyone you interact with. Also, visualization is not the same thing as wishful thinking, especially when it comes to money. Just because you fantasize about having more money doesn't make it a viable outcome. Making money is the means, not the end.

A true outcome, one that inspires a shared passion, is one that others have not yet imagined. It is unique in some definable way. It has distinct value, both to the ones who imagined it and those who end up benefiting from it. It can even be based on previous ideas. Edison's original light bulb was the fulfillment of his passion-fueled objective, but the LED bulb was a new outcome based on an old idea. Such an outcome may seem obvious in hindsight (good ideas usually are) but are often considered strange or audacious at the time. Modern technology has many such examples.

By the early 1980s, IBM dominated the mainframe computer market. However, the company was seeing its position eroded by lower-cost minicomputers and was troubled by the emergence of even smaller microcomputers like the Apple II. Determined to launch its own personal computer in this growing market, IBM's team, headed by the late Philip "Don" Estridge, was operating under severe constraints. The mandate was to develop the product in an extraordinarily short time frame—six months. To make matters worse, IBM's policy was to use only components and systems developed by IBM internally.

Despite this, Estridge and his team persuaded the company to allow the use of non-IBM components. This novel approach, unhindered by past experience, allowed them to visualize a new objective—one that helped IBM successfully dominate the market for the rest of the 1980s.

However, the truly audacious objective in the IBM PC story was that of a then-obscure Seattle company called Microsoft. It's founders, Bill Gates and Paul Allen, had heard of Estridge's project and set out to become the developer of its core operating system.[35] Not content merely to license MS-DOS to IBM for a one-time fee, they envisioned a different outcome: the requirement *to include their operating system on every PC sold*! They also sought to make the agreement nonexclusive, freeing Microsoft to license DOS on other companies' personal computers.[36]

IBM agreed, and their audacious idea became the foundation of Microsoft's immense financial success. Even when IBM's product gave way to dozens of imitators, the ongoing royalties from DOS and its successor, Windows, far exceed anything that Gates and Allen could have secured with a one-time deal.

To be sure, their vision did not guarantee success. They were admittedly nervous when the plan was proposed. They made their audacious proposal knowing it was a risk and not knowing if it would even work. But the fact remains that they did not allow past experience to prevent them from setting their sights so high. Too many of us stop going for our vision because of fear of failure.

That singular objective became a shared passion throughout the company and has helped Microsoft weather the ups and downs of the tech market for decades. Today, Gates and his wife have applied the same audacious strategies in the 2000 launch of the Bill and Melinda Gates Foundation, reportedly the world's largest private charitable foundation with over $46 billion in assets.

— *v* —

A more recent example of starting with a clean piece of paper is the late Steve Jobs's original vision for the iPhone.[37] Before Apple's announcement, the smartphone category included a number of devices, such as Research In Motion's BlackBerry, that were extremely difficult to use for tasks other than phone calls or texts. Each of these devices had a physical keyboard, a small screen, a camera, and a severely limited web browsing capability. However, Jobs did not want to create a device that merely competed with existing smartphones;

he envisioned an entirely different outcome.

After more than two years of development, the original iPhone was launched. It was a combination of Apple's popular media player, the iPod, a 2G phone, and unfettered browser access to the internet. It abandoned physical keyboards and styluses in favor of a touch-screen interface and Apple's signature visual approach to information. The combination captured public imagination. It was a major factor behind Apple's increase in net worth—from $82 billion in 2007 to over $2 trillion at the end of 2020. What was Jobs's secret? *He did not allow past experience to limit his thinking.* Other well-established phone manufacturers had developed similar phone-with-a-keyboard devices that included many popular features, like easier texting and email, but they had failed to gain mass appeal. Jobs and his team took time to PAUSE and visualize something other than a conventional smartphone. They shared—and were passionate about—a different objective, namely, "the internet in your pocket," and proceeded to find creative ways to make that happen.

— *v* —

The role of a leader is to find out where *everyone* in the group wants to go, from the members of one's team, to the people they serve, and everyone in between. To do that means identifying the outcome that makes sense to everyone and then removing the obstacles that prevent such an outcome. Such a destination can be audacious and seemingly out of left field. It requires creativity and courage to think beyond past experience and limiting thoughts. It also requires persistence. Our negative thoughts, distractions, and fears will not magically just go away, so we must continuously reinforce a mindset to counter that natural drag and resistance.

Above all, having a compelling objective requires conviction and confidence, and the practiced ability to PAUSE, as often as needed, and take out a clean sheet of paper. When we have that clear destination—or destiny, if you prefer—and hold it with the passion it deserves, we will begin to achieve true velocity.

07 YOU DON'T HAVE ALL THE ANSWERS

IN SWIFT'S FAMOUS SATIRE, HIS CHARACTER Gulliver discovers a strange, flying island called Laputa.* Its inhabitants claimed to have all the answers—to *everything*. However, they were incapable of speaking (or anything else) unless a servant periodically tapped them with a special instrument or wand. Swift was mocking the intelligentsia of his day, but he also was making a point. *People who are ineffective and unhelpful tend to think they have all the answers up front.*

They do not—and neither do we. In fact, thinking that we do is a huge barrier to gaining velocity. If we want to lead others, and if we want to have speed and direction toward an ideal outcome, then we have to be okay with not having all the answers up front.

It's not easy. Most of us *do* have useful knowledge and experience, especially if we've achieved something great in the past. Success

---

* Jonathan Swift, Gulliver's Travels, (London, 1726). Don't confuse Laputa with Lilliput, another of Swift's fictional countries filled with ridiculous, narrow-minded inhabitants.

doesn't happen by accident. But when we have a new objective—that ideal outcome we visualized on that clean piece of paper—we're in uncharted territory. If that goal is audacious, then it will require solutions that are largely unknown. The last thing you need is a set of preconceived notions and reasons why it won't work.

— v —

In 1962, President Kennedy made his "We choose to go to the moon" speech at Rice University in Houston.[38] In the speech, he famously declared the ambitious goal of landing a man on the moon within the decade. At the time, the United States had already put a man in orbit and had sent an unmanned probe toward Mars. But the idea of putting a man on the moon and bringing him safely back seemed fantastic. We didn't know exactly how it could be done!

At the time, there were several conflicting theories on how to do it. There was also an undercurrent of fear, uncertainty, and doubt. The potential cost was enormous, both financially and politically. Neither Kennedy nor the NASA scientists knew all the answers beforehand.

Regardless, Kennedy put forward the idea, which captured people's imaginations and planted an indelible, ideal outcome in the minds of decision makers, administrators, and engineers. Once begun, the process led to NASA discovering new solutions—followed by more and more solutions—culminating in Neil Armstrong's famous first step in July of 1969.

As with any big idea, there was no guarantee of success. There were tragic miscalculations, including those that killed three astronauts in 1967. But they learned from their mistakes and were always willing to admit they didn't know everything up front. Former NASA engineer Dr. Henry Pohl described the mindset that ultimately led to the program's success. "The kind of attitude back then," he said, "was that when you had a problem . . . you did what you needed to do to find a solution to it. You didn't throw up your hands and say, 'I can't . . .' or 'It's not . . .'" Not knowing the answers up front was not only permitted, but it was also essential to achieving the objective.

Pohl credited the program's success to the team's relentless focus on the goal—beating the Russians to the moon. But he also pointed out the importance of their attitude toward failure. "There are times when failure is not an option, but *if you're not allowed to fail, then by definition, you cannot succeed.*" (Emphasis added.) "We were able to get things in test early, prototypes, even things we knew sometimes wouldn't work, but at least it gave us an idea of how to change something, modify it, how to do something different."[39]

The power of the initial thought, voiced by Kennedy in 1962 and pursued by NASA personnel with persistence and focus, resulted in a large group of people uniting to achieve a single, remarkable outcome.

— *v* —

If we don't have the answers up front, then where do these big ideas— these ideal but audacious-seeming outcomes—actually come from? In his 1910 book, *The Science of Getting Rich*, author Wallace Wattles argues that there is an unlimited supply of such potential. It resides in what he describes as the Formless Substance, the "thinking stuff from which all things are made, and which, in its original state, permeates, penetrates, and fills the interspaces of the universe."[40] In order for that to take tangible form, he argues, one must consciously apply *thought*.

> "A thought, in this substance, produces the thing that is imaged by the thought. Man can form things in his thought, and, by impressing his thought upon Formless Substance, can cause the thing he thinks about to be created."[41]

This does not mean that you can simply *will* success into your life. Wattles's idea of a Thought in Formless Substance is not based on wishful thinking; it's not a belief based in feelings instead of evidence. Rather, success is the result of first directing that thought toward an unknown but very real potential.

Wallace goes on to describe the process as primarily creative, not competitive, since the potential for that Thought in Formless Substance is unlimited.

> "You are to become a creator, not a competitor; you are going to get what you want, but in such a way that when you get it every other man will have more than he has now . . . Remember, if you are to become rich in a scientific and certain way, you must rise entirely out of the competitive thought. You must never think for a moment that the supply is limited."[42]

The notion of unlimited supply may seem foreign in the competitive, zero-sum world of business. In sales, for example, competitors often resort to out-bidding one another to win a narrowly defined goal. This reduces the entire conversation to one of pricing, where nobody really wins. But the supply of creative opportunities really is unlimited, as I discovered when I switched from selling copiers to offering a better communications vehicle, as described in chapter 1.

In business, going into a situation with preconceived ideas is indeed a narrow, zero-sum game. But the creative approach, one that requires an open mind and willingness to look for gaps and new ways to benefit all parties, is one of unlimited potential.

In order to gain velocity, we must hold that audacious idea in our conscious thoughts, every waking hour, even without knowing the answers. However, this does not mean we should get so wrapped up in the idea of visualizing goals that we fail to act on them. If the objective is clear and compelling, then we have no choice but to focus on its fulfillment.

> "The more clear and definite you make your picture then, and the more you dwell upon it, bringing out all its delightful details, the stronger your desire will be; and the stronger your desire, the easier it will be to hold your mind fixed upon the picture of what you want."[43]

This act of continuous, conscious thought will lead to new questions and new answers which, when acted upon, turn that audacious thought into reality.

The concept of a Thought in Formless Substance assumes, fundamentally, that we do not have all the answers up front. If we think we do, then we are not shooting high enough. Success and wealth go to those who are first to find new roads, not to those who copy the actions of others and stay in their comfort zones.

This mindset was fully in force with the Apollo project engineers, as it was more recently with the original iPhone team at Apple. When a new or unexpected problem arose, the statement, "I don't know the answer," was an acceptable first response. In fact, it was often the important first step in discovering a solution.

In both examples, the compelling nature of the objective was powerful enough to overcome resistance and pull team members into alignment. It made it more likely that someone confronted with a problem would PAUSE, consider the issue from many angles, ask questions, and express their resolve: "I don't know, but I can find out!" It produced sustainable velocity.

— *v* —

Often, in today's business world, it is difficult for people to imagine that Thought in Formless Substance—that ideal outcome. The culprit is usually our own illusions that we somehow already have the answers up front. It can happen without conscious thought but, tragically, it can prevent us from attaining velocity.

In the last chapter, I shared some of my dealings with a chemical manufacturer faced with a dilemma. You recall the pioneer developer of a cost-saving reagent for the copper mining industry: they were under threat from competitors who drastically undercut them on price—for an inferior but similar reagent. I had asked the principals of my client's company to visualize their ideal outcome, without allowing their past experience to constrain them. After the "clean piece of paper" discussion, they found their true objective. It was a negotiated, ten-year contract, locking in 75 percent of the market, rather than a bid against others for a three-year contract.

I told them that securing a negotiated contract would require a different set of actions than those involved in the bidding process. Their next question was very logical, "How are we going to *do* that?" But my answer was not what they expected; I said, "I have no clue."

As you can imagine, they were startled. But I was serious. I explained that I did not presume to have all the answers up front. It was their business. However, I was confident in the fact that the outcome they wanted was achievable. Intuitively, I knew they were doing less than 20 percent of what it would take. So I said I knew they were capable of doing more—that they could achieve that outcome.

After some candid discussions, they were convinced they could trust me and begin the journey. It's never easy. Even with such a powerful, compelling objective—that Thought in Formless Substance—taking that first step is hard, but important. Once you do, the idea takes form and becomes reality.

Once that trust was established, we identified the key players, the information we already knew, and the information we didn't know yet. I met with the team on a quarterly basis and, over the next six quarters, we met to evaluate the information they uncovered, which led to more questions, which led to new ideas. This all led to a growing team awareness as to *how* they could motivate their customer to do things in a new way.

As the team became genuinely focused not on the sale but on their *customer's* ideal outcome, they opened up, revealing more about their problems. Each encounter prompted creative ideas for solving these previously unknown issues, as both sides began acting collaboratively, developing strategies to make those solutions real. As the copper mining company's confidence in my client grew, the relationship changed. My client's status changed from being a minor supplier to that of a partner critical to their success.

In the end, my client succeeded in securing a negotiated ten-year contract. More important, they had become partners in generating velocity for both companies.

— *v* —

When it comes to the execution of any plan, the first step is the most important. Clearly stating that one compelling objective—without claiming to know all the answers—is critical. It may not happen exactly the way you had in mind, but without that initial Thought in Formless Substance, it will not happen at all. Think about every successful venture you can imagine, including your own. It started with an objective so clear and compelling that it led to a stream of questions:

- "What does it look like—in detail?" (The vision question.)
- "What do I need to *do* to make it happen?"
- "Who do I need to enroll or recruit to make it happen?"
- "What resources do I need to make it happen?"
- "What is my timeline for making it happen?" (Things don't get done without a time deadline.)

The subsequent, practical steps of executing any plan all come from this initial idea and the questions it generates.

I'll give you another example. In 2011, I was voted president of the National Speakers Association, which is the beginning of a four-year cycle. Beginning as vice president and then president-elect, I was slated to become president in 2013. It was a singular honor, but I knew that once you become president, your time is no longer your own. I would be representing the Association throughout the world, and I knew that I would have less time for my own speaking engagements. Knowing that this would adversely affect my income, I had to prepare a backup strategy.

I needed to create a line of revenue that would utilize my skill sets but that also fit my new situation. I literally did not know *any* of the answers up front, so I began to search. Fortunately, I soon attended a seminar for speakers on how to create their own mastermind group. Masterminds, as you probably know, are high level, peer-to-peer mentoring groups of like-minded professionals looking to grow their skills and their businesses. I had personally benefited from them over the years.

The idea was intriguing. I was familiar with masterminds, but until that moment, I had not considered them as a revenue stream for my business. I thought, "Paid mastermind. What would it look like? What do I need to *do* to make it happen?" And so on. I knew it worked for entrepreneurs, but would it work for corporate America, for executives of small to midsize businesses? I pondered these questions for a time until, one day, I had a striking conversation with a friend—a well-known sports executive. During our typically intense conversation, he said something unexpected. "I'm the GM of this team," he said, "but who can I talk to? Do you think the president or the league wants to hear my problems? I can't share it with my players. Who do I talk to?!"

That startling admission gelled something for me. People I worked with—sales VPs, CEOs, and others dealing with revenue issues—didn't have people to talk to! They couldn't share their fears with their direct reports or their investors. They needed a peer group where they could share freely and work out issues in confidence.

That was my Thought in Formless Substance! I had been puzzling over how to start a meaningful mastermind group within my own field and wondering if anyone would consider paying for it. My friend had answered the question without my asking! That gave me the confidence to write a one-page summary and, at a subsequent gathering of executives, began sharing the idea. It resonated with others. Before I knew it, I had my own organization, the CRO (Chief Revenue Officer) Mastermind Group, which is thriving to this day. This relatively small group allows (or rather *requires*) members to be vulnerable and brutally honest (in a caring manner) with each other, and practice true peer-to-peer mentoring in a confidential environment.

Some of the members even started to retain me directly, having connected and become more comfortable with me during our sessions.

None of this would have happened if I had entertained all my negative thoughts and allowed them to derail that original Thought. I certainly did not have all the answers about paid masterminds, but I kept asking questions. I allowed that Thought to stay in my conscious mind and, suddenly, my friend literally gave me the answer.

— *v* —

The difference between people who have ideas but do nothing and those who succeed with their ideas is that the latter *are willing to be comfortable not having all the answers up front*. Being comfortable with that reality is the only way to forge new ways of dealing with existing problems.

So how should we apply this idea to our challenges as leaders? Here are some recommended steps:

Take any problem you are currently dealing with. (If there are lots of problems, pick the one that's keeping you up at night.) Start with the vision, the ideal outcome to the situation, written on a clean sheet of paper, as we discussed in the last chapter.

Let it sit in your conscious thought every waking hour. Turn it over in your mind and get comfortable with the fact that you don't know the answers.

As you think about it, *you'll start asking yourself new questions*. (You'll know they're the right questions because they're not about why something can't be done or was never done before.)

Look for the answers to the new questions. Very often, they will come from unexpected sources. This will put you on the path to velocity.

Just before my daughter was born, my ex-wife and I started talking about baby carriages. This had never entered my mind before—ever! But all of a sudden, that idea triggered something in me. I began to see baby carriages everywhere! I certainly didn't have any answers, but I was asking the questions.

That's what it's like with a Thought in Formless Substance—one so audacious and powerful that it precludes the notion of having all the answers. If you let it into your conscious mind, keep it there every waking hour, and start asking the right questions, you'll be amazed at what happens next.

08 TASK VERSUS PURPOSE

IN LEWIS CARROLL'S CLASSIC, *ALICE'S ADVENTURES IN WONDERLAND,* the main character finds herself participating in a "caucus-race." It is led, appropriately, by a dodo bird. In the race, Alice and the other characters "began running when they liked, and left off when they liked, so that it was not easy to know when the race was over." Carroll was probably poking fun at certain people known for running around in circles, getting nowhere—namely, politicians.[44] However, the story illustrates a bigger point. *People everywhere engage in tasks that have no connection with a meaningful outcome or purpose.* When they do this, the result is speed without direction, leading to burnout and, inevitably, loss of velocity.

This problem affects many different kinds of would-be leaders. For sales professionals, performing tasks without purpose takes the form of focusing on the *features* of a product or service (the "how" part of the equation) without ever considering a prospect's ideal *objective* (the "what" part).* For CEOs, it can come from a business initiative based on past conditions, assumptions, and limitations, rather than on an ideal outcome—one that starts with a clean piece of paper.

For people in general, whether they have a leadership title or not, tasks without purpose can be any of the whirlwind of daily routines that sap our enthusiasm and numb us to the possibilities around us. A task may feel good emotionally, in the moment, because it feeds our need for perfectionism or goodism. Neurologically, our brains crave certainty, and a sense of control.[45] The hormones resulting from completing a task, oxytocin and dopamine, give us a positive emotional reward. However, if the task itself does not support a *bona fide* outcome, then the neurological reward is only a short-term fix. Such a task will simply create drag and resistance—the opposite of velocity.

Getting caught up in tasks without purpose usually happens without warning. We rely on routines all the time to deal with all the urgent needs of the day. It's hard enough to find time for matters labeled "important and urgent," much less the objectives that are "important, but not urgent." It's a problem of prioritization. For many reasons, people forget to focus on what is critically important to achieving an objective. They get lost in nuisance tasks because they're easier or more familiar or more interesting in that moment. It's all too easy to let our habits and past experience limit our thinking. We're only human.

Contrast that behavior with what Halford calls the five Cs: certainty, choice, control, completion, and context.[46] Prioritizing and completing the *right* task, one that supports an ideal, sustainable

---

* See my previous book, *Lead, Sell, or Get Out of the Way* (Hoboken, NJ: John Wiley & Sons, 2009).

outcome, will trigger the same positive feelings, but those will last a lot longer, because they have greater meaning and purpose.

— *v* —

Thankfully, it is possible for leaders to overcome this resistance, regain an active awareness of their ideal outcome, and prioritize tasks that support their purpose. In fact, they can do this not only for themselves but for others on their team.

One of the first steps is to realize that *everyone needs to experience a sense of control* in their work as well as life in general. It's a profound, psychological need, rooted in our evolved survival mechanisms.[47] The uncertainty and unpredictability experienced when you don't have control of your environment triggers a fight-or-flight (cortisol) response. To find examples of this, look no further than the anxieties we all have experienced in the wake of COVID-19. Its unpredictability, unknown duration, and disruptive effects created a shared feeling of loss of control and anxiety nearly everywhere. Such emotions make it harder to consider long-term outcomes and easier to stick with routine tasks—even those that don't support your purpose.

Long before COVID-19, one of my clients experienced a perfect example of this problem. His production supervisor had stormed in one day, complaining that so-and-so (a welder) was always on his cell phone and was constantly late in finishing his work. When asked what the supervisor was doing about it, the frustrated, angry answer was, "I told him to get off the damn cell phone!" This had produced exactly zero results, other than frayed tempers. It was out of control. The employee continued his unproductive behavior, despite already having this difficult conversation. In fact, both of their cortisol-fueled emotions probably made inappropriate tasks inevitable. To the employee, talking on the phone, however unproductive, was something that gave him a feeling of control.

So I suggested a different approach, using a role-playing exercise. I asked, "As the supervisor, what do you know about this guy?" The answer was that he wanted to become a master welder. To reach that level, one of the prerequisites was to produce work on time. So the supervisor's role-play discussion centered on the employee's aspirations, the quality of his work (which was good), and what it would take to make up for delays in his work.

When this approach was applied in real time, the subject of cell phone use never came up. Instead, the discussion was about the employee's objective and coming up with tasks supporting that purpose. Both were more engaged and motivated, and both regained a greater sense of control. The unproductive tasks were not curtailed by external threats or the emotions behind them. They changed because both of them found the intrinsic motivation to achieve a desirable outcome.

When having a conversation with someone with an opposing viewpoint, the object is not to change their viewpoint by force. Rather, the object is *to elevate the conversation to a higher want*, a desired outcome that both parties want to achieve. By doing so, both sides are motivated to work toward a solution. This is what is necessary for any leader in the US government to move forward a country that is as deeply divided as we have seen in the 2020 US presidential election.

By fighting the battle (the problem of cell phone overuse), the supervisor was losing the war (the need for higher productivity). By shifting the conversation to a shared vision, getting the employee on track to becoming a master welder, they stopped focusing on the wrong issue. Rather than being diverted and off-track, they recalibrated themselves to the important issues in a way that motivated them both.

— *v* —

The solution to unproductive tasks is never to merely prohibit them. Ask yourself how successful you were with a diet or an exercise regimen merely by saying to yourself, "Don't eat that doughnut!" or "Stop loafing on the couch!" Having someone else say it (or shout it) isn't any better. Doing a purposeless task, even a self-destructive one, gives us a short-lived sense of control and completion. If we are not motivated by a better, more compelling outcome, then just yelling "stop" will not change our behavior.

Unfortunately, many managers expend a lot of energy and emotion trying to *change* other people. By this, I mean they want others to be more like them, which rarely goes over well. (When I talk about this publicly, I jokingly ask, "Who wants to be fixed?" which gets exactly zero raised hands.) Such managers are doomed to failure, fighting the wrong battle over tasks that support no real purpose rather than winning the war.

The problem is that *they are trying to manage the tasks instead of managing the results.* A leader properly focused on the results knows that he or she does not have all the answers up front. The reason to bring others into the picture is that they will see things differently. They may have different ideas as well as solutions you hadn't thought of, in which case they should be allowed to pursue new tasks to achieve the results more quickly. If someone's actions are counterproductive, they must be addressed, of course, but only if the purpose is to manage the results.

A leader's job is not to change people. It is to understand what motivates them, to know their aspirations, and to create an environment where they can be productive, doing the tasks that support a common purpose. This is not always easy. When someone is moved or promoted within a company, their native skill sets—the ones that helped them succeed in performing purposeful tasks in the past—are not always aligned with new tasks and responsibilities. A leader must always know whether or not a team member can learn to do *new* purposeful tasks.

I had the privilege of working with a large telecommunications company whose management had asked me to evaluate their sales force and find out why some were performing well and others poorly. I found that their top 10 percent performers were predominantly extroverted and task-oriented. They loved to socialize, and their success was a direct result of their actions. However, the bottom 10 percent performers tended to be introverted and process-oriented. I asked if these low-performers had been great at customer service and had been rewarded by promoting them to sales. They all had.

Management had been trying to change these people without knowing their intrinsic skills and motivations. They had excelled at customer service positions, where process, people, and attention to detail were paramount. But once promoted to positions requiring different tasks, they lacked the temperament and motivation to succeed in a results-oriented sales role. They failed because they were moved from a seat where they excelled to a seat for which they were not suited.

Entrepreneurs and CEOs are only human. They care for their people's welfare and are reluctant to fire or demote. But their emotions lead them to err, "parking" someone in an unsuitable position out of reluctance to deliver bad news. Instead, they should always start with the end in sight and then work backward to find the most suitable person to accomplish the necessary tasks.

The late Jack Welch, CEO of General Electric, earned the nickname "Neutron Jack" (after the neutron bomb) because of his reputation for eliminating people while leaving buildings intact. His "10 percent" policy meant that every year the lowest performers at GE were simply let go. As cruel as this may sound, it actually liberated many people to find situations and tasks better suited to their passions. Some achieved great success and thanked him for creating the new opportunity.

— *v* —

In describing the dynamic of motivation and productivity, I am indebted to the work of author, trainer, and consultant Judy Suiter.[48] Her work in behavioral science and organizational development have greatly impacted human resources training, team building, and professional communication. With her blessing, I have adapted one of her concepts to helping CEOs and other aspiring leaders achieve greater velocity. This is a tool I describe as Productivity Alignment.

Productivity Allignment

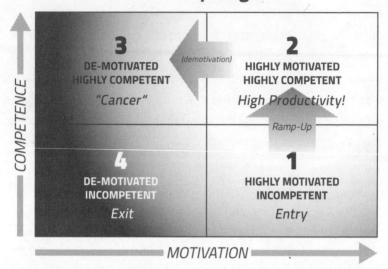

In any organization, there are varying levels of both competence and motivation. Those who are just starting out are highly motivated but not yet competent in their required tasks. (See the first quadrant, above.) A ramp-up process is required in order to achieve the necessary competence (the second quadrant). This ramp-up can be haphazard in some companies, but eventually these people begin to perform well. Their tasks support the purpose that motivated them to join in the first place.

Unfortunately, this does not always last. Some people shift from being highly productive (motivated and competent) to the "cancer" zone (the third quadrant). They are still competent but no longer motivated. There are several reasons for this. Their job may have changed, and they are no longer a good fit. Someone else may have been promoted over them. Their reasons may be personal or financial. Often, they believe, rightly or wrongly, that they are not valued or respected.

Regardless of the circumstances, these people are no longer aligned with the company's central purpose. Increasingly, their tasks will be contrary to the organization's purpose, and they may recruit others to do the same. Like actual cancer, their unhappiness and lack of alignment will metastasize, leading others in the department or organization to pursue tasks at odds with the desired outcome or purpose. Left unattended, such demotivated individuals will in fact become incompetent, since they no longer desire to pursue the tasks that support the organization's purpose! Despite their past experience or success, they will end up in the fourth quadrant by default.

A leader's choices are not easy or pleasant in this situation. Ideally, they may ask the right questions—to discover that person's aspirations and find a way to restore their motivation, as my client did in the case of the welder who would not stop using his cell phone. But there are occasions where tough decisions are required.

Leadership decisions of this nature are a tightrope walk, balancing the desire to help a colleague with the need to maintain overall velocity. Ultimately, when such individuals persist in the "cancer" zone, either they will eventually leave themselves feeling totally demotivated, or you will have to belly up to the bar and make the difficult decision yourself.

— *v* —

One of the major challenges faced by any leader is the tendency of others to interrupt and interfere with your vision, your ideal outcome, by imposing arguments and demands related to their own needs. These interruptions usually trigger a cortisol-fueled, emotional response. The resulting battle does not result in actions that support *anyone's* objectives, and only serves to create more drag and resistance in the situation.

As with many challenges to velocity, these situations can apply to personal situations as well as business. My own experience illustrates this problem in detail. It began as an unwelcome interruption.

In June 1988, while driving through the Lincoln Tunnel, I received a "call service" message on my car phone. (For those of you under thirty, car phones were brick-sized behemoths physically bolted to the inside of your vehicle.) After I cleared the tunnel, I called the answering machine and listened to two irate messages from one of my aunts. My mother had apparently been involved in a horrific accident, but she knew little else. I then contacted the Fair Lawn Police Department in New Jersey, where I had connections from my days as an EMT. They didn't know her condition, but they knew the accident was bad enough for her to be sent to a trauma center in Hackensack.

Months earlier, my father had been diagnosed with a terminal condition, with my mother becoming his primary caregiver. She had hired some help but kept working full time. The demands of work, caregiving, and concern for the future had made her chronically fatigued, so I knew anything was possible.

I was on full alert as I raced to the trauma center. Upon arrival, I learned that my mother had passed out at the wheel. Her car had jumped the sidewalk and severed a light pole, with the jagged edge puncturing the gas tank. The car caught fire in front of a Porsche dealership. Seconds after she was pulled from the car, it exploded, taking out the entire dealership. She was in critical condition, with third-degree burns on 30 percent of her body.

Talk about cortisol being out of whack. All I could think about was how was I going to deal with my mother's condition *and* with my terminally ill father. For two days, I was living out of my car, trying to deal with both parents, their doctors, lawyers, employers, the destroyed Porsche dealership, and insurance companies. In the midst of that chaos, I actually did the "clean piece of paper" exercise, stating my ideal outcome. It was that no matter what happened, both parents must survive. I did not want to live with the knowledge that one parent did not make it because I fell short. The trouble was, I had no idea how that could be accomplished.

Family members came to the rescue, as is often the case in bad situations. They provided welcome respite (and dinner) but also a singular challenge.

My mother's older sister, a take-charge aunt whom I affectionately call "the General," had flown in from San Diego. At the dinner table that night, after my two-day frenzy of activity and worry, she made it clear that caring for both parents was too much. She thought I should concentrate mainly on my mother, the one who had a greater chance of survival.

The argument to prefer her sister did not sit well with me. I loved the General, but was sorely tempted to scream, "How dare you make me choose between two parents!" I wished my arm were long enough to reach across the table the shake some sense into her. Fortunately, this was all in my head, and for no more than a few seconds. I recalled my yet-unfulfilled ideal outcome and realized that I was on the verge of fighting the battle (over winning an argument) but losing the war to keep both parents alive. I needed her help, so I had to build a bridge fast, unifying both our motivations.

I told the General, "I cannot imagine the thoughts you are having with the potential loss of a sister. I believe it is close to my thoughts of possibly losing a mother. But when Miriam (my mother) wakes from her coma, what do you think is going to be her first thought?" After a pause, she replied, "How is your father?" I offered that if she knew my dad was no worse off because of her accident, then she might be able to use that energy to heal.

From that point forward, we worked together as a team. The great news was that my mother survived after three skin graft operations and resumed her career. My dad managed to hang on for another year.

Many of you have gone through similar, life-changing challenges. They can be intensely personal, professional, or, as we're experiencing with COVID-19, a combination of both. Some are more detrimental than others, but all share a common theme. The old saying is true. It's not what happens to you that counts, but how you deal with it. As the leader of your own life, your organization, or your family, it is important to deal with the emotions of situations properly and not let them cloud your judgment and lead to bad results.

The issue is not that others are interfering with your vision—something they cannot do unless you allow it. Nor is it the side battles that pull you off course and prevent you from reaching the desired destination. The issue is that your vision of the desired outcome is not clear enough or engaging enough to keep you focused on the goal.

When you are clearly focused on the ideal outcome, however, it becomes possible to deal with unexpected interruptions and interference—even when the short-term consequences are damaging. A few years ago, I was on a three-city tour delivering keynotes to the sales force to kick off the new year. The VP who hired me shared this story. As the regional manager in California working his way up the corporate ladder, he had a top-performing salesperson who posed such a challenge. He was responsible for 60 percent of sales in his territory but had increasingly become a distraction to the rest of the team. He had become extremely self-focused, making demands to satisfy his own ego. He exhibited the signs of the "underchallenged" form of burnout, described in chapter 3. He had low stress levels, unlike his peers, because he found the work unrewarding. In essence, he was a typical example of a top producer becoming bored, moving from quadrant two (high productivity) to quadrant three (cancer), potentially drawing others into his sphere. He also thought no one would ever do anything to him because he was too valuable to be replaced. Boy, was he in for a rude awakening.

The regional VP was faced with a tough decision—one that carried substantial risk. But he knew that his ideal outcome would not happen if the situation continued to contaminate others. So he fired his top-performing salesperson, even though it cost a lot of business that year. However, eventually he grew the territory's business, an accomplishment that launched him into senior management. The resulting velocity would not have happened had he not taken a bold step, however risky, with a clear vision of the objective. It also brought life to the old saying, "No one is irreplaceable."

— *v* —

Engaging in tasks that fit the desired outcome is never a one-and-done process, whether you're acting as an individual or as the leader of a complex organization. The COVID-19 crisis proved definitively that our best-laid plans can be interrupted or even obliterated. The question is how we get through the emotional turmoil of the battle and apply ourselves to the tasks that are meaningful *now*.

You must constantly ask the important questions:

> **"Is the vision itself still valid?"** What was once clearly a compelling ideal outcome may no longer apply to a world in constant change. As the COVID-19 crisis proved, altering one's vision, or recasting it entirely, is always a possibility.

"Are my present tasks the right ones, and am I prioritizing them correctly?" There will never be enough hours in the day, so prioritizing the most important ones is essential.

"Am I executing these tasks in the best way possible?" As we will explore in future chapters, there are better ways to listen, trust in your instincts, and act in ways that optimize velocity.

Adapting to changing conditions is the ultimate touchstone for determining if our tasks support our purpose. If we fail to adapt to a changing environment, it will become impossible for others to join us in completing these tasks.

A while ago, a company I worked with, a manufacturer of fabric used in things like bandages and tea bags, was trying to secure a major deal. They had done their due diligence in excruciating detail, and created a highly polished, compelling presentation. Unfortunately, in the week preceding the presentation, the prospect had drastically changed its corporate initiatives and instituted a total restructuring. The presentation went off without a hitch, and the customer praised its thoroughness and quality but told them it was now completely irrelevant. Their task had become meaningless.

The conditions in our world, and our perceptions of that reality, are changing daily. Exceptional leaders know this and do everything necessary to stay on top of their team members' goals, issues, and roadblocks. They know when to alter the task when it no longer serves the purpose. Failure to do so minimizes our relevance and ability to influence others. But doing so accelerates the velocity of the entire team.

Our brains are predisposed to want control and completion of the tasks we undertake. Rather than be satisfied with just checking a box, however, we need to up our game and prioritize those tasks that are relevant to our quest for greater velocity.

09 THE ROLE OF INTUITION

HUMAN INTUITION IS NOT ALL THAT magical or mysterious. Psychologists describe it as knowledge that manifests in our conscious mind without obvious deliberation.[49] It's part of our evolutionary heritage. Our ancient ancestors who *sensed* danger quickly were simply more likely to survive than those who stopped to think about it first. As a result, we all have the ability; it's part of our brain wiring, so to speak. When used properly, intuition is also a key part of gaining velocity.

Our intuition is not perfect, of course. It lets us do many complex things more or less unconsciously—like driving to the store once we've learned how. Sometimes, it helps us "read" an encounter with someone, even before we've heard all the facts or gotten to know them well. But our "gut feelings" can also mislead us. As Nobel laureate Daniel Kahneman so thoroughly described,[50] our automatic, unconscious thought process can be the source of cognitive errors or biases, such as priming, the halo effect, and confirmation bias, which can result in bad decisions.

Here's an example you can identify with. Recently, I was driving to a meeting at a location that was new to me. It was on a freeway I had traveled very often, but at a different exit than I usually took. You can guess what happened next. Because I was not paying attention, my mind chose the exit I was familiar with, which of course was the wrong one. It was a classic case of an unconscious decision that was both quite normal but incorrect.

However, despite the risk of "autopilot errors," our intuition *can* be the source of valuable, even inspirational new insights and solutions to problems, especially if we have *bona fide* experience and expertise in a particular area. Intuition involves unconscious pattern matching, something that our brains do naturally. So if the information we have to work with is accurate, then it's more likely that our intuitive flashes will be valid. Again, that doesn't mean our expert intuition is perfect, nor is that of other experts, but it *always* merits our attention.

— *v* —

So how can we make better use of our natural intuition to achieve velocity in our personal and professional lives? In my consulting and public speaking on the subject, I frame the discussion on intuition and velocity using the three basic words advocated by one of the world's premiere communication and executive leadership development coaches, Paul Dominguez. Those words are *listen*, *trust*, and *act*. They can be summarized as follows. We need to:

Listen, contrasted with hearing others' words and interpreting them from your own point of view.

Trust, without the precondition of having all the answers up front.

Act creatively, being willing to execute decisively on what you intuitively know—on behalf of the person you're listening to and ultimately on your own behalf.

Listening, as opposed to merely hearing, is the hallmark of every good leader. By "hearing," I mean that the words someone says reach the hearer's ears, and their brain receives the signal but immediately tries to truncate and fit it to the world as they see it. That is not effective listening. It's a form of *confirmation bias*, where the listener already has an idea or concept that they *want* to be true and therefore seek out only that information that they feel supports it. They hear the words but unconsciously sort and reinterpret what the words mean to fit their own narrative.

On the other hand, real listening happens when the listener *consciously sets their own notions and assumptions aside* and puts themselves into the world of the person who's talking—hearing the words from the speaker's perspective.

It's a fact that people use certain words based on their own biases and experience. So it's vital that we hear others' words not in the context of *our* biases but as they were meant by the speaker—so that we can understand *their* biases. This makes it easier to raise the conversation to a higher level, one that is aspirational for both parties.

A good way to tell if you're listening or not is to check if you're looking for "your turn" to say something during a conversation. If you're already forming your next statement in your head, then the chances are good that you're hearing the other person's words but not actually listening.

In chapter 3, I recounted an experience with two different companies, both of whom were looking for a motivational speaker to help their sales organizations cope with the Great Recession of

2008–2009. My own speaking schedule had dried up considerably, so when they both called within a twenty-minute interval, I thought, "Ha! The Recession is over!" Had I merely heard their words and fit them to my own narrative, I might have said yes to both gigs. But in the long run, I knew it would have reduced velocity for someone, including me, so I asked what they meant by the word "motivation."

As I listened, the first executive made it clear he wanted entertainment and diversion, to improve the morale of his people in tough times. Twenty minutes later, the other executive also said that times were tough. But then he said he wanted to give his people all the tools necessary to outperform the competition. They were both in the same predicament, with the same need, but were worlds apart with their emotional wants.

In both cases, I was able to raise the conversation to a level that benefited both parties. I referred the first executive to a fellow speaker who specialized in entertaining performances. The other's need was directly aligned with my strengths, so we proceeded to arrange the event. Listening produced greater velocity for both companies as well as myself.

Listening always involves getting into others' biases—to understand their true wants. When we hear ordinary words, especially those that are common to our particular industry, we must stop making assumptions. These are often incorrect because they are based on our own biases.

For our book on customer service,[51] we included a case study on a major auto rental company and how they created an industry-leading brand. During an interview, one of their executives related a story that illustrates the peril of making assumptions. In a survey of top renters, one issue involved dissatisfaction with how long it took to return a car on their way to their flight. Company executives heard this as criticism of the bus runs between the depots and the terminals, so they increased the bus run frequency, only to receive the very same complaint six months later!

This time, they really *listened* to their customers to understand *their* perspective. When they did, they discovered the problem was not with the bus ride but with the time involved in waiting in line for a receipt. The subsequent creative thought resulted in the now-familiar, belt-mounted devices used by agents in the parking lot, who could now print a receipt on the spot.

Interpreting customer's words according to the executives' experience and biases prompted them to ask the wrong questions and come up with unproductive answers. But listening to the words in the context of the speakers' point of view produced the opposite—a solution that met everyone's needs.

— *v* —

Listening is not limited to the words and perspectives of others. It also means *listening to oneself*, which is where intuition plays a major role. Many times, we are at a loss in a given situation. We don't know what to do, but our subconscious mind is still at work sorting through accumulated experience and information, pattern matching, and processing—all without our volition. It may not produce the right solution every single time; our intuition can be imperfect or even misleading at times. But this process—our intuition—is the actual source of our Thought in Formless Substance described in chapter 7. When it's right, it can result in lasting velocity. So, just as it's important to listen to others' words in the context of their assumptions and wants, it behooves us to do the same for ourselves.

There are barriers to this process. Being task-oriented—driven to getting things done and done *right*—is an admirable leadership trait when used in moderation. But it can also be overdone, leading to perfectionism and indecision. Even when an intuitive idea is worth pursuing and validated by knowledge and experience, we are often impeded by our limiting thoughts, as described in chapter 2.

The solution to this impasse is to PAUSE, take a deep breath (or several), and ask, "What do I need to do here?" Invariably, the answer will come from two sources: the heart or emotions as well as the mind. Once you ask the question, however, the answer usually comes quickly. Intuitively, you will already know the right thing to do, and the response is clear. You may not have enough historical data to form the perfect answer or satisfy your desire for a greater comfort level, but you still need to *trust* your intuition and *act* decisively.

Our instinct does not necessarily produce the right answer every time, but it has been shown that our instinctive *confidence* in our answer is a reliable indicator.[52] If it takes us too long to assess a situation in our mind, then we may be adding too much clutter to what our gut intuition is telling us.

Whenever I am making a tough decision, I am prone to perfectionism—making "perfect" the enemy of good and dragging things out interminably. But when I consciously ask my intuition what I should do, the answer comes quickly, and I have learned to trust it. It is not always right, but more often it is. More importantly, it moves the needle, versus being stuck with no decision. Time is money, after all.

Over the years, my experience with CEOs and business leaders has revealed an interesting pattern. When the question of *what to do next* comes up, they fall into one of two modes:

If the answer comes slowly, with significant hesitation or lots of verbal dodging about, then their limiting thoughts, their perfectionism, and their past experience are fully in play—preventing them from moving forward toward an ideal outcome, *or . . .*

If the answer comes quickly, as the first thing that enters their mind, then they are listening to their heart or "gut." Their intuitive answer may or may not be correct, but they are in the best possible mode for attaining velocity.

When following our intuition, we have to trust that our decision will work with the confidence of knowing that if it doesn't, we can tweak and adjust it. Trust is the antidote to the feeling that we must have all the answers up front, which in turn creates drag and resistance. Trust and action results in success and increased velocity. However, if the action is unsuccessful, velocity is not impaired, because failure reveals problems sooner than if we succumb to stalling and delay through lack of trust.

Creative action is the ultimate outcome of trusting our intuition. It is the substance of the decision-making process that we will explore in the next chapter. It is also a frequent topic in my work with CEOs and other leaders, especially in the uncertain times stemming from COVID-19. When a situation is new and unpredictable, it is quite common for even experienced leaders to vacillate. Their tendency toward perfectionism is heightened, and their caution can be overemphasized to the point of stifling creative thought and decisive action. It is then that we need to PAUSE, ask the basic question, and choose the intuitive course of action.

— *v* —

Our intuitive response to other people involves sensing patterns in their behavior, whether we're consciously aware of it or not. This is enhanced when we interpret the data using *all* our senses—especially the combination of sight, sound, and touch. In my sales training days, I always observed greater success when my clients met their prospects in person than when they relied solely on email or a phone call. Using only a single sense always makes it more difficult to "read" the other person and sense their response intuitively. To optimize one's intuition in a given situation, it is best to access as many data points as possible.

By the way, the use of Zoom and other video conferencing platforms can partially accomplish this, as we learned during the pandemic, but it requires that we pay attention to what's on screen. As much as 85 percent of our message is sent through body language, so it's possible to miss a lot during a Zoom meeting, making it more stressful and harder to fully engage.[53]

I have had many opportunities to put my intuition and the ability to read others to good use. In chapter 8, I briefly described my work with a major telecom provider, where I had identified some of the personality characteristics of their top-performing and low-performing salespeople. But when I submitted my proposal for the project in person, a decision made based on my training in behavior styles, I encountered unexpected resistance.

I had assumed that, like me, the senior manager was task-oriented and interested in moving forward quickly. But it turned out that he was far more analytical in his thinking and required substantially more information before proceeding.

As I sat in his office at first thinking I had nailed the proposal,

I noticed he was being fairly silent—not objecting to my plan but also not showing any enthusiasm. I could tell from his facial expressions and body language that something was wrong. Trusting my gut that things were not going well, I knew that I had to act decisively, knowing that there would be risk involved. I stopped the conversation, ripped the proposal in half, and said, "You're not buying this, are you?" to which he said, "Exactly." I then asked him to share where I was off the mark.

His whole demeanor changed, which I read as a positive response. After listening to his concerns about the validity of the behavior assessments and whether they would result in a solution, I began the process of satisfying his need for more data, including a statistical analysis of the model's accuracy. In the end, he approved the project, but I would never have had the opportunity had I not trusted my intuition, asked the question, listened to the response, and acted decisively.

— *v* —

Listening is also about being *present*. People you talk to will usually know whether you're really there, actively listening to what they're saying and considering their perspectives, or off somewhere in your own biases and preconceptions. When you are fully present, the conversation is always more productive and more likely to meet the needs and aspirations of everyone.

In some of my seminars, I would conduct an improv game called, "Building a Story, One Word at a Time." Based on a suggestion from the audience ("ocean," for example), the six participants would have to build a story, one person and one word at a time. The first would say, "The," followed by the next saying, "ocean," followed by "is," "blue," and so on. What I found was that when people were not being present—unaware of what was being said, assuming what was going to be said, or just thinking about something else—they paused for a *long* time before saying a word. They often did what nonlisteners do: changed the conversation to what *they* wanted and negated what was said before. But those who were present almost immediately had the next word and continued in the flow of the story.

Fun and games aside, when this happens in the real world, there are consequences. When someone only hears the words and fits them to their own assumptions and preconceptions, the conversation usually ends. The other person shuts down, stops listening, and can even walk away. Cortisol levels increase and, in the end, velocity is lost. But when the listener is consciously present, actively seeking to understand the speaker's assumptions and biases, the conversation flows, providing space for trust and decisive action.

The cost of not listening, trusting, and acting is enormous. We make assumptions about things others say and do, but those assumptions are often invalid. Think about any time in your past when someone made a statement about you, and you perceived it as wrong, to the point where it bothered you. Suppose you waited weeks before trying to clear it up. How much time did you spend on that *assumption* of what was said? How did it affect your mood and your productivity, taking time away from other concerns?

Some time ago, I conducted a nonscientific survey of my colleagues, asking them to estimate how much time they spent during a year dwelling on assumptions of this kind. The numbers varied, but the average was *between three and four weeks* spent on tasks that didn't make sense because their assumptions were wrong. This included unproductivity because of impact on their mood or attitude or simply the unproductive conversations or time-consuming activities that these assumptions generated. What would you be able to do with an extra three or four weeks in every year?

— *v* —

When I began my career as a sales/leadership coach, it was hard to entertain what I felt were fuzzy notions or "fluff" about intuition. To tell the truth, I was more arrogant and cared only for black-and-white business results. But thanks to intuition experts like Nancy Rosanoff and executive coaches like Paul Dominguez, I began to see things differently. There was an undeniable connection between one's intuition and the success or failure of the business at hand.

I learned that when I let the fear of potential loss get in the way of me listening, trusting, and acting on my intuition, I usually experienced worse results. So now I just listen, trust, and act on my intuition.

Always remember that your sense of the facts should be as equal as possible to that of the other person's. If it is not, and you are working on unvalidated assumptions, then your intuition will not perform for you in the way you would like. Your intuition is not infallible, but when consciously practiced, it will help you attain greater velocity.

10 PROBLEM SOLVING WITH THE END IN SIGHT

IN THE PAST FOUR CHAPTERS, we have discussed the nature of your destination—or destiny, if you will. It starts with visualization: literally writing the ideal outcome on a clean piece of paper, from scratch, without any regard for what you believe is possible, and not based on past experiences. That ideal outcome is your true destiny, the focus of your passion. You will not have all the answers up front. The secret is to find that audacious goal and hold on to it while continually seeking out the right tasks—and the right people—to make that goal a reality.

To do this well, you will be *solving problems and making decisions* on a continuous basis, which is no small task. It is hard to keep our past actions and preconceived ideas from leading us down unproductive paths. This does not mean you haven't learned valuable lessons in the past, especially those learned from past failures, as we discussed in chapter 4. These can indeed guide us in avoiding known pitfalls. What it *does* mean is that, when solving *today's* problems, we must not let the decision-making process be limited by past experiences. If we do, it will cloud our thinking of what is possible and what is not.

Problem solving is not limited to your pursuit of that audacious goal. It is for any outcome you're looking to achieve, whether it's the outcome of a meeting, a project, or a year's productivity. It's also essential when you need to find the right people to help you reach your destination—people who won't be easily demotivated and pulled out of alignment.

This process will involve all the subjects discussed in this book, especially the process of executing your velocity strategy (chapter 12). But before we move on, let's look at problem solving itself.

First of all, problem solving should not be a linear process. We're tempted to make it so because we experience life in chronological order, as cause and effect, so we're used to seeing things as a single, straight line. We read books and watch movies from start to finish, so we're inclined to approach narrative decisions the same way. The difficulty with solving problems in a linear manner can be demonstrated with a math riddle:

How do you make this formula correct?

24 − 14 = 2

RULES: You can't change or re-order the numbers. The minus and equal signs must stay the same.

The nonlinear answer is to represent the numeral four as an exponent instead of an integer. Subtracting fourteen from sixteen (two to the fourth power) now produces the right answer! The problem just had to be viewed differently.

Always start with the end result.

$$2^4 - 14 = 2$$

Then look at the problem
from a different point of view!

The secret to execution is making effective decisions—and just like solving the math riddle—it is achieved by looking at the desired end result and then thinking differently about the steps needed to get there. In chapter 4, I described Stephen Shapiro's account of an airport dilemma over excessive wait times at baggage claim. Rather than look at the problem from only one angle (speed of baggage delivery), they viewed the problem from *every* angle. They looked at the ideal outcome (satisfied passengers) and asked what could be done differently to achieve that outcome. Once a creative solution was realized (making the passenger walk to baggage claim more enjoyable but slower) the solution was obvious.

When you know the ultimate destination, finding the right answers on how to get you there do not need to happen in sequential order. In fact, doing so can often bring you to a standstill—bogging you down in old ways of thinking and losing the context for what that step really means. Having the right information, even when viewed "out of order," impacts your ability to achieve the best outcome.

The book you're holding now is an example of this. When

I approached my publisher about doing a book on the velocity mindset, he was skeptical at first. I explained the concept, a leadership book that was also a self-help book, which he said had not been done before. I had a clear idea of the intended outcome, but he was not fully convinced. So we brought in an editor and produced a detailed outline, one that changed as we made decisions and fleshed out the details. Once he was on board and the writing was underway, I still did not make decisions in a linear fashion. At one point, I wrote two later chapters, 12 and 14. These defined the goal of the book further. With that end in sight, I was able to write the intervening chapters more easily, with a clear objective to guide me.

Believe it or not, creative decision-making often works out this way. When Stephen Spielberg or Aaron Sorkin create a film or television show, they never shoot the scenes in the order the viewers see them. They start with a vision of the final result. Then, each decision is made on its own merits, looking for creative and unexpected solutions to a particular scene—but always with the context of the end product firmly in mind.

Another benefit of thinking in a nonlinear fashion is that we can break down a big decision into smaller ones. Earlier, I described the daunting prospect of renovating a run-down building in a sketchy New York neighborhood. Nineteen out of twenty who saw the potential chose to drive on by, thinking the problem was just "too big" to consider. But that one individual who saw potential *and* acted accordingly did something crucial. Working her way backward from the desired outcome, she broke the problem down into smaller, key milestones—each one creating a measurement benchmark. With these in place, whenever she realized results were not proceeding as planned, she could evaluate the situation and make better decisions on how to proceed, always with the final destination in mind.

— *v* —

Making decisions can be difficult. It can be hindered by our fear of failure, which we express (under the guise of collecting more data) in the form of procrastination. As we discussed in chapter 4, we are also prone to perfectionism and goodism (the need to prove our worth) and other limiting thoughts. It just feels better to play it safe and make no decision at all. But as businessman and venture capitalist Ben Horowitz once said, "Often any decision, even the wrong decision, is better than no decision."

So then, how can we break the logjam in ourselves and make meaningful decisions, solving problems on the way toward achieving our ideal outcome? The answer can be summarized by asking these four questions:

Am I looking at the problem from all possible angles? As we discussed earlier, problems are more difficult to solve in a linear fashion, so the steps or decisions should always be viewed with the end in sight.

What does my intuition tell me? Having the necessary information is always a good idea, but there will come a point where your intuition, backed by knowledge and experience, must be the decisive factor.

What are the possible negative outcomes—and can I recover and/or learn from them? Any decision can have unintended consequences such as failure; risk is a fact of life. A leader must not let fear of failure derail the decision-making process or forgo the potential to learn from mistakes.

Does the decision address a symptom or a root cause? Too often, people respond out of emotion and only address the symptoms rather than the root cause of a problem. By reacting instead of getting to the real source of the problem, the same issue will crop up repeatedly, even though it may look different.

This applies to even the most consequential decisions you can imagine. In the situation room at the White House, the president has access to vast amounts of relevant data, analysis, and expert opinion. But ultimately, he or she cannot allow fear of failure to postpone or derail a major decision during a crisis. After all the information is presented, the guiding factors must include intuition and a passion for the ideal outcome. Of course, you don't need to be the president, or even a CEO, to follow these principles. They apply to leaders of every kind.

Informed intuition and a healthy regard for possible outcomes are essential to making decisions that ultimately produce velocity. Not long ago, a client brought me in to help with their largest account, who had been battering them on price to the point where the business was no longer profitable. Even the high sales volume from the account did not allow my client to make their numbers.

When I met with their VP, I said we could go through the process I had followed in other divisions of the company. I also said that for this to work, both companies had to have the same values, but if they didn't, there was a good chance of failure. I asked if they were prepared for the consequences of it not working out. He said yes, and we proceeded to approach the client with a new business proposal based on value, not price. Unfortunately, after three months, my client not only lost the new business but also a significant amount of their old business.

Later, when I voiced my disappointment, my client's VP confided that, despite the loss, he had known it was the right decision. The way things were going with that account, he knew, deep down, that their dealings were already headed in the wrong direction, and that ultimately, they were going to lose the business. However, they made the right decision. Intuitively, he knew it was right to leave no stones unturned while at the same time knowing they may fail in reaching the desired outcome. It hurt, but it was an outcome he could live with. More important, it forced the company to pivot, evaluate who they were, and decide how they would achieve their long-term goals.

We all have doubts about making these decisions; too often, they prevent us from making them. The solution is to consciously ask the question, "What is the worst case if I make this choice?" Very often, it is something, however unpleasant, that will not prevent you from attaining your ultimate goal and will likely be an occasion to learn. Remember that even a wrong decision is often better than no decision. The trick is to keep moving forward.

— v —

Many times, people make decisions about the wrong issues. They are dealing with outward symptoms rather than the root cause, affecting overall velocity. This can happen because of the emotional sense of urgency in a situation, whether an immediate decision is warranted or not. We feel the emotional pressure to address a symptom rather than a root cause. Cortisol levels are spiking, in ourselves and those around us, and our instinct is to *do something, now!* Unfortunately, this can result in a decision with only temporary results or worse. It can bring us back to the same place we started, a vicious circle of action, reaction, and no progress toward the ideal outcome.

The answer to making meaningful decisions is always to dig deeper—to uncover the reason for lack of progress toward the real destination. Doing so requires looking at the problem from many angles, asking questions that uncover others' needs and objectives, and always keeping the conversation focused on achieving the right outcome.

There is a touchstone to remember for any intuitive decision you've made, despite any doubts and whatever the outcome. That is whether or not you can go home at night with the confidence that you made the choice, the one that was true to your vision and values. If you proceed with the information you have, trusting your intuition rather than waiting for the "perfect time," then no matter what the outcome, you will be creating velocity for yourself and your team.

As we'll see in part III, there are many problems to solve and decisions to make in order to align ourselves and our team to achieve a velocity mindset. Before moving on, however, now would be a good time to PAUSE and take stock of the lessons learned in previous chapters. Think about all the possible steps you'll need to take to achieve your audacious goal. The chapters that follow will give you the toolset for doing so more effectively.

03

ACHIEVING ALIGNMENT

11 THE ART OF LEADERSHIP LEVERAGE

WHENEVER YOU HEAR THE WORD "LEVERAGE" in a conversation, you may think of the finance definition, "the use of borrowed money to increase production volume, and thus sales and earnings."[54] You also may remember the business definition, "the ability to influence a system, or an environment, in a way that multiplies the outcome of one's efforts without a corresponding increase in the consumption of resources."[55] I am talking about something different. *Leadership* leverage does indeed involve influence and a multiplication of efforts, by people in addition to yourself, to achieve a desired destination. *True success is not a solo act.* You can only learn and earn so much from your own efforts; you can do so much more with the efforts of others around you.

This is not a cold business process; it is deeply personal and relational. No matter how well you handle your own limiting thoughts or how well you can visualize an ideal outcome, your success will be limited without the help of others. Those others can include customers, vendors, investors, market influencers, and even friends and family members. Leadership leverage involves identifying and cultivating others—those with the skill sets you do not have, or those who may be referrals or sources of influence on your behalf. In each case, you will be facilitating their capacity to attain velocity as well as your own.

Benefiting from the efforts of others is not a new concept, of course. A friend of mine recently left his position at a prestigious law firm to start his own relatively small practice. He did this despite being in line for partnership. So in my usual "soft-spoken" NY manner, I asked him, "Are you crazy? *Why the hell* would you make such a move?" His answer was simple. At his former firm, he said, he would only keep a portion of the return for his labors. As the head of his own firm, he would receive not only compensation for his own work but also for a portion of the work done by those he brought into the new firm. I knew it was not just about the money. He needed others to augment the ideal outcome for the new endeavor. To do so, he had to retain colleagues who shared that vision. He also knew he also had to facilitate them and their ideas in order to sustain that velocity.

Leverage can take many forms. In sales, a top producer may believe that her success depends mainly on her own efforts, while in reality it's all about the efforts of those who support her. This understanding becomes critical when that person is promoted to a sales management position. She will succeed not only on her own efforts but also on those of her team. Her job is not to do the team members' jobs for them but to identify gaps, ask questions, and otherwise equip them and follow their progress. Her job is also to run interference for the team, using her leverage to remove roadblocks so the salespeople can concentrate on connecting with customers, ascertaining their needs, and selling effectively. This is also true for any manager or leader of a team.

Not everyone put into a position of leadership fully realizes this. In chapter 1, I described a top-performing sales rep, who I'll still call "Bob." He was elevated to national account management but clearly did not grasp the principles of leadership leverage. Basing his actions on his previous experience, namely jumping in to fix every problem at a moment's notice, he utterly failed to support his team, depriving everyone of velocity. His real job, and the heart of leadership leverage, was to identify and assess the gaps in his people's conduct, coach them in better behavior, and monitor their progress.

Leadership leverage can be organizational as well as personal. Entire companies can leverage one another's strengths to their own mutual advantage. Distributors can independently represent companies that don't want or cannot afford a direct sales force, providing more "boots on the ground" and a prebuilt network of customer relationships. Airline alliances are another example of using leverage to maintain or increase their market leadership. By sharing mileage awards, easier connections, and other benefits, each member airline of groups like Star Alliance, SkyTeam, and Oneworld improves their own business velocity with the assistance of the other partners. They can claim to fly anywhere in the world, even to places their own planes do not go.

Leadership leverage is about *expanding your effectiveness in achieving goals through others*. These are individuals, teams, or other entities who either complement your organization or provide the missing skills or structure necessary to meet those goals. Such leverage occurs when we learn how to ask the right questions, unbound by past experience or fear of failure. In chapter 4, I recounted how a major airport resolved the problem of excessive complaints over wait times in baggage claim. Rather than focus on the urgent, cortisol-fueled anxiety over "too-slow baggage delivery" (a financially insoluble problem), the team PAUSED to consider a different question: how to reduce wait times. They considered the problem from a different angle, so they might *leverage* each other's expertise in passenger flow—not baggage flow. The entire team's collective creativity was leveraged to arrive at the right answer.

When you ask and *answer* these questions, you will be able to *take decisive action* based on the exercise of *intuition* and a willingness to acknowledge your own biases and weaknesses. Everyone on your team, including you, is prone to making decisions on the basis of past experience and assumptions, as we discussed in chapter 9. But when you actively listen to the needs and concerns of others on your team, or of your customers or partners, the intuitive answer will become clearer—increasing the odds significantly that your decision is the correct way to proceed.

— *v* —

Nowhere else is the concept of leadership leverage more clearly seen than in building alliances through the process of obtaining referrals. In *Lead, Sell, or Get Out of the Way*, I wrote that building alliances was one of the seven traits of great sellers. But the concept itself is far more than good sales technique. Leaders must leverage relationships of many kinds, not limited to seeking for potential customers or strategic partners. Referrals are often essential when trying to recruit top talent—those with the skills and ideas needed to accomplish an ideal outcome. But no matter what type of alliance or benefit is needed, there is a right way and a wrong way to obtain referrals.

Almost every day, you can observe the *wrong* way—in the emails or phone calls you receive from naïve, overeager salespeople. After pitching a product or an idea you had no intention of buying, or even if you are already a regular client, they will invariably ask if you know someone else in your department, your company, or your circle of influence who might be interested in their product or service.

The same thing happens at certain types of networking events. Don't get me wrong. Networking is the name of the game, but it should be about mutual sharing of ideas and building new relationships. Unfortunately, there are events labeled as networking where the main object is to poach candidates with the best resumes, seek out referrals, or convince someone to recommend you. Their participants have lost sight of the mutual nature of networking and turned it into a self-focused task. This does not serve them well. It's true that people like to brag about the vendors who make them successful, but it should be their idea, not yours. Ask yourself why someone who said they would refer you doesn't do so. Could it be your positioning?

Picture yourself at a cocktail party or other gathering where you find yourself in conversation with a potential influencer—let's say, a noted attorney with an excellent reputation for a certain type of litigation. If your own practice is different from theirs, you might be tempted to ask, "If you have any clients I could help, please refer them to me." The response will be underwhelming. But what would happen if you switched your focus to them, asked them about their business, and actually showed interest? In effect, you're asking about their "brand promise" to clients. Then ask how your expertise might help extend their brand promise. It's no longer about you, although you may end up with a referral. It's about helping them.

Referrals, in their best form, are opportunities to mutually share and benefit from others' knowledge and experience. They move the "ask" from being self-focused to being an offer of help. They are also the most effective way to find the best talent, those people with the skills, intelligence, and intuition needed to accomplish an audacious goal. A lucrative sale or a critical hire may occur through such referrals, but these are *byproducts*, not the reason to cultivate these relationships.

Referrals are not only about finding the right talent. Think about the common notion of "six degrees of separation," where everyone on Earth has only six social connections with every other person. When you make a connection with someone—by seeking to help them, not principally yourself—you are making a potential connection with everyone on the planet, including those who can facilitate your ideal outcome!

According to some, scientific studies indicate that there may be fewer than six steps involved due to the impact of social networking.[56] Think about that the next time you try to get a referral. Your approach, good or bad, can potentially reach every other human being.

Classic examples of good referral networks include peer-to-peer networking groups like Vistage International[57] and the Young Presidents' Organization, founded in 1950, with a membership of over 29,000 executives in 130 countries.[58] These groups are known for open sharing of information and experience, even among competing companies. Members are not there to sell but to help one another and be helped in return. Some trade associations function on a similar principle, offering events and publications where leaders can learn and share the latest information. They may also make deals and acquire new talent, but seasoned trade event participants do so as a secondary activity—the *result* of their participation, not the main reason to attend.

On a smaller scale, my own Chief Revenue Officer (CRO) mastermind group has a similar effect when it comes to leadership leverage. One member, the head of a plastic packaging manufacturer, stated it this way:

> The group dynamics that every member of the CRO experiences are powerful. Through the dialogues of the entire group, we garnered the lessons of others that we could apply to our situations—the successes AND the failures.
>
> We found support in one another, but more importantly, we were able to leverage the safe environment to hear the brutal honesty that is essential to our personal and professional improvement.
>
> The CRO is marketed around sales, but it is truly a leadership development experience. Today, our sales have increased as a direct result of the CRO. The entire company has developed knowledge and skills on how to interact more effectively and gain velocity in all that we do.
>
> —Brian Tauber, CEO, CPP Global

Referrals and relationships develop when the main object is to give more than you seek to gain. From my experience as a sales/leadership coach, and especially during disruptive times like the COVID-19 pandemic, I found that the best formula for sales professionals and other leaders is to always make *help* calls, not *sales* calls. As I discovered in my time as a copier salesperson, find the real issue of concern, instead of immediately jumping in with a sales pitch. Ask questions and actually listen to the answers without preparing to spring the trap, so to speak. Your intuition will lead you—and the person you're working with—to a creative solution that benefits everyone. This idea transcends sales and is the essence of leadership leverage.

— *v* —

When considering the concept of leverage, or of velocity in general, there are two different "modes" to consider. You can be emphasizing:

Working IN the business—being focused on the internal, day-to-day problems that we all must face, or

Working ON the business—making the connections and leveraging the ideas and talents of others to accomplish an ideal outcome.

Of course, it's impossible to ignore the details of any viable business. However, executives and managers who are overfocused on being *in* the business become myopic, viewing every process and person as a separate problem to be solved and unable to consider the outcome. They are more *task*-oriented and tend to take their eye off the big picture. Everyone on their team is worried by their particular task. The leader is concerned with the big picture and concerned how today's actions will affect the future, both immediately and over the long term. The CEO's job is never to micromanage tasks. It is always to manage the *outcomes* of their direct reports, who in turn do the same thing with others below them. That releases the CEO to work *on* the business, to leverage relationships with other leaders and with partners, influencers, and customers.

Working *on* the business is entirely different. Despite the necessary details, such leaders are looking forward, considering the future of the business. They constantly ask questions like, "Where is the market headed?" or "What do I (we) need to do to keep up?" and "Do I have the right talent to make it happen?" They seek the ideas of like-minded individuals and leverage those relationships, increasing their capacity to make intuitive and very often productive decisions.

It's easy for executives to fall into the trap of working *in* the business instead of *on* it. Entrepreneurs and founders of small businesses have had to do a lot of the heavy lifting by themselves, without the luxury of others helping them achieve their vision. But at some point, when the company grows to the next level, they can fail to transform to the CEO's leadership role. Instead, they continue to act like a founder or entrepreneur, stay deeply involved in the microdetails, and wonder why they can't achieve greater velocity.

All this applies not only to CEOs but also to division and department heads and line managers. Out of necessity, they must deal with the details in their tasks. However, as leaders, they must also focus on the business at a higher level, looking ahead to achieving the ideal outcome.

— *v* —

Like-minded individuals may agree on the outcome but not necessarily on how to achieve it. A big challenge for leaders occurs when they hire people to implement best practices but nullify that effort by telling new hires, "That's not the way we do things here." In contrast, *successful leaders manage the results, not the "how" part.* They leverage their employees to find the best ideas to get there—one of the guiding principles of Lean.

It may be that a leader's intuition will kick in, informing them that a particular "how" is not achieving the outcome. They may then push an employee to fill in the gaps, but they must never quash new ideas. Once they do, fewer people will take risks to present new ideas. When an organization loses that kind of mutual leverage, it will cease to be competitive.

The hiring process, as we discussed in chapter 8, is a prime example of leveraging the right people to achieve an objective. However, the process can be hindered by a too-narrow, subjective focus. This happens when the executive in charge of hiring relies on intuitive feelings based on what the candidate *says*, even when they have objective, assessment-based information. Out of a sense of urgency, they may stop looking and hire the first person that checks enough boxes, literal or emotional, without considering any other candidates. Instead, they need to pay attention to potential red flags, often coming from assessments, that may result in future problems. A leader can then balance those with their subjective feelings, ask better questions, and gain information and insights that will either validate of counter their feelings. This process is critical to ensure that their intuition is on the right track and not leading them down a path to failure.

Not following this process leaves the door open to confirmation bias and a lack of transparency between the executive and his growing team. It can also lead to disaffection and demotivation by the new hire—someone who was only nominally aligned with the CEO's real purpose. Ultimately, that leads to the employee's drift away from productivity and into a "cancer quadrant" situation. (See page 92.)

— *v* —

In many cases, a dynamic CEO or the founder of a company or organization, regardless of their title, is their best salesperson—period. They have the passion for the company's ultimate destination, and their job, by definition, is to be focused *on* the company and its velocity, not only *in* the company and its workings. For example, Virgin Group's founder Richard Branson and mobile tech giant HTC's cofounder Cher Wang are famous for drawing in people and leveraging their talents to undertake striking initiatives. Their focus and that of their people is *on* the business more than *in* it. And, in the case of Branson's Virgin Galactic division, it is literally out of this world.

On a more down-to-earth level, there are other ways that leaders can productively leverage others. One of these is a speech or presentation. Of course, not all CEOs or presidents are confident enough to give speeches to large crowds, but those who do find enormous opportunities to exercise leadership leverage. As a professional speaker, I have observed that the most effective speeches are given by leaders who *helped* the audience rather than tried to *sell* to them. Not only did the audience discover something enlightening or practical, but they also formed a connection. Just as the salesperson who makes a *help* call rather than a *sales* call, the leader who joins an association and presents genuinely helpful ideas, unconditionally, is more than likely to find a partner, a new hire, or an engaged customer, after the fact.

— *v* —

No matter how thoroughly you have mastered the previous concepts in this book, you will not attain significant velocity, for yourself or for the organization you lead, without the active involvement of others.

As human beings, we are wired to achieve things in the context of groups, with members contributing according to their own needs. With such mutual leverage, we can accomplish objectives far greater than the sum of individual accomplishments—without diminishing the value and meaning of those individuals.

In the chapters that follow, we will explore some of the means by which this leadership leverage is accomplished, including the techniques for executing our velocity strategy.

12 MOVING FORWARD, EXECUTING YOUR VELOCITY STRATEGY

AS ANY BUSINESS EXPERT WILL TELL you, executing a strategy for change is the most significant challenge any leader will face. The odds are not good. According to McKinsey & Company, 70 percent of change programs fail to achieve their goals, due to employee resistance and lack of support by management.[59] I should add that the problem is not limited to resistance by employees. Our own limiting thoughts and narratives can keep us from executing a strategy for greater velocity.

Strategy execution qualifies as a hot topic among CEOs and executive coaches, given the high stakes involved in achieving—or failing to achieve—successful innovation. Business analysts pay little attention to great new ideas unless at some point they result in financial growth. Likewise, practical execution is also the hallmark of self-help advocates and coaches. The stakes for growth and achievement are as high for people as they are for companies. If you are "stuck" personally, unable to move forward with your life because of misconceptions or self-limiting thoughts, then your business interests will be impacted, and not in a good way. Likewise, if your team is mired in self-focused tasks without purpose, unable to clearly see and work toward that one ideal outcome, then your personal life and health is likely to suffer.

Current thinking on how to improve strategy execution is divided into two schools of thought, according to Michael Mankins, a managing partner at the consulting firm Marakon Associates.[60]. One school emphasizes people. According to Mankins, "The idea is you get 'A' players, you pay them a lot of money, and you pay them for the performance they generate—irrespective of what may be happening in some other business or region." The other emphasizes process rather than people, a view championed by former GE executive and Honeywell CEO Larry Bossidy.[61] This school maintains that organizations don't go out and hire bad people; something else must be getting in the way. But Mankins concludes that both propositions have merit. "I think [both schools are] just two sides of the same coin," he said.

Leadership is the key to effective execution, but that leadership has to be personal as well as organizational. You can't be an effective leader of an organization without being a leader of your own life—and vice versa. Our efforts to implement velocity are interrelated, whether it's on an organizational level or a personal level. This holds true whether you have a leadership title or not. As stated in the first chapter, leadership is not about your *position* but about your *disposition*.

Bossidy maintains that, to get things done, a leader must master certain essential behaviors[62] if they are to excel at execution and avoid becoming micromanagers. These include things like knowing your people, insisting on realism, and setting clear goals and priorities. But the last one, "know yourself," clearly highlights the need for a leader to achieve their own personal velocity.

"It takes emotional fortitude to be open to whatever information you need, whether it's what you like to hear or not," Bossidy writes. "It enables you to accept and deal with your own weaknesses, be firm with people who aren't performing, and to handle the ambiguity inherent in a fast-moving, complex organization."[63]

So how can someone develop this kind of emotional fortitude? Some of it is part of our native temperament, to be sure, but a great deal comes from our ability to overcome limiting thoughts and critical self-narratives, as discussed in chapter 2. This mindset can also be reinforced when we learn how to respond to cortisol-producing situations, by focusing on others' objectives at least as much as our own. Above all, our emotional fortitude can be strengthened by trusting in our intuition and being comfortable the fact that, without a doubt, that we do not have all the answers up front.

— *v* —

Successful execution of a velocity strategy requires the existence of three important leadership qualities:

Integrity. Only those leaders whose actions consistently embody commitment to stated principles and goals will inspire others on the team to act the same. One's personal ethics also have lot to do with one's integrity.

Accountability. Mistakes happen. Execution does not always go as planned. When a leader owns those mistakes, their credibility grows. This impacts the hiring process as well as their ability to lead those hired into meeting future objectives.

Celebration. The success of any stage of execution is cause for celebration. Leaders who foster it as a normal result of their team's culture and remain empathetic to their team members' goals and aspirations are far more likely to keep their team moving toward the desired outcome with greater velocity.

— *v* —

The first requirement, integrity, is cited often in leadership books—for good reason. If sound principles and goals are to be effectively implemented, their advocates must actually put them into practice, in their own lives as well as in company practice. To do the same, others on the team must see a leader's demonstrated commitment to the outcome.

Unfortunately, people in positions of authority can talk a good game but too often fail to walk the talk. They fall into the trap of "do as I say, not as I do," allowing past actions and assumptions—and their resulting tasks without purpose—to derail their own personal velocity as well as its overall implementation. This is impossible to hide from others. When an executive's actions belie their words or when their talking points are formulaic or clichéd, it creates drag and resistance for the entire team.

This was brought home to me in an encounter with a large medical imaging manufacturer. I had previously delivered a well-received keynote address to their newly merged sales force, so their senior VP brought me in to address a huge issue. The merger brought together two companies with disparate cultures, creating a new $2 billion entity. He was struggling on how to bring these two cultures together. He asked me to come up with ideas that would help them become a unified, effective team.

The presentation did not begin well. I began to describe the principles I had taught successfully in the past, like value-added selling and key account strategies. But he immediately interrupted, "Stop!" He turned to his lieutenants and asked, "If he talks about that, what will be the reaction of the team?" They all went thumbs down. After a few more such attempts, I stopped my presentation in frustration and asked what was really going on. His management and sales force had responded well to these concepts in the previous event. Why would the newly combined force now find them unappealing?

His answer brought up a powerful point. The team had heard such ideas from previous speakers but had seen little or no follow-up or support from management. Senior managers were too tied up with day-to-day crises (tasks without purpose, I realized) to spare the time on meaningful change. Given the magnitude of the merger and importance of bringing everyone into alignment, he could not afford to have just another "flavor of the month" as the speaker. "I need to find a unifying presence, a process that brings the two cultures together, quickly," he said.

What he was seeking from me was not sales training or sales skills. He needed a process that he and other executives could get passionately behind to unify the two company cultures. What he wanted was a unifying process. And then he said, "You know, there is this great book out there called *The Titan Principle*," referring with a smile to my first book. "What I want to do is leverage your process to unify the team. To raise the team above the emotional fracas that the merger has caused to a result that both sides aspire to." He went on to say, "I cannot afford to do what we always do, which is bring in a speaker and never follow up on their ideas. Failure is not an option here. I need perfect execution!" This is a big issue with management, and a key reason why execution fails. *No matter how brilliant or insightful an idea may be, if management does not follow up and support it along the way, others will not follow, and the idea will fail.*

The good news is that integrity works, as many successful CEOs and entrepreneurs have proven. John Hall, CEO of Calendar Inc., wrote, "Share your leadership message with your team; if you've written something down, let them see it. Let them know what you're trying to achieve with your leadership message and ask them to stay aware of it—*and call you out if you slip up.*"[64] (Emphasis added.) As we see in world events unfolding today, transparency is also a key part of integrity.

— *v* —

The second leadership quality necessary to execute a velocity strategy is accountability. When leaders are transparent and accountable for their actions, our instinctive response is to be drawn toward their stated purpose and to support it with our actions. Transparency, or the lack thereof, can make or break one's velocity. Of course, this is easy to do when the results are positive. *The real test of accountability comes when mistakes occur*—as they always will.

Take two famous examples of company accountability. In 1982, a series of poisoning deaths in Chicago shocked the country and put one popular brand in jeopardy. The victims had all taken Tylenol capsules that had been laced with cyanide! Johnson & Johnson, the manufacturer, responded immediately. Without waiting for the outcome of criminal investigations, the company removed and destroyed the product on store shelves, shut down its Tylenol production lines, and publicly offered to replace (for free) all purchased Tylenol capsules with tablets, at an estimated potential cost of $80 million.[65] Mindful of their "doctor safe" brand promise, the company publicly acknowledged the situation, announced their actions, and promised not to bring the product back until it was considered safe. The company's market share plunged from 35 to 8 percent during the months-long crisis, but rebounded in less than a year, thanks in part to public perception of its response. (To this day, safer, tamper-proof packaging is also the results of this crisis and Johnson & Johnson's public accountability.)

The key is acknowledgment, not necessarily taking blame. We live in a litigious society. People sue others many times for no real reason. In its actions, Tylenol did not say it was responsible. What they did was acknowledge the issue that the brand, because of outside events, was no longer "doctor safe." They took the brand off the shelf. This kept intact the brand trust that was built over many years. So when the product reappeared as "doctor safe," customers believed them, and the business resumed. Acknowledgment is the first step in conflict resolution. If you don't acknowledge others' pain up front, even if you have the right solution, people will not believe you because they feel you don't really understand their situation. Accountability involves owning up to the reality of the situation.

Contrast this level of accountability with that of ExxonMobil after the *Exxon Valdez* grounding in 1989, where over ten million gallons of crude oil were poured into Prince William Sound in Alaska. When Exxon persisted for months in denying accountability for the incident, public outrage grew to the point where many cut up their credit cards in protest, and the company's reputation suffered. Because of Exxon's sheer size and influence, it did not suffer long-term economic consequences from their lack of accountability, but imagine the effect of such behavior on a smaller company.

Examples involving *personal* accountability (or its absence) are common in the world of politics. In 1998, President Clinton's denial of the Monica Lewinsky relationship resulted not only in his impeachment for perjury but also a shadow of mistrust, even among his supporters. Although he escaped some of the scandal's consequences—most notably his impeachment trial acquittal—his lack of transparency diminished his ability to execute effective policy changes.

In contrast, when President Kennedy had to account for the disastrous Bay of Pigs invasion, his response was memorable. Kennedy seized on the power of the new medium, television, to say to the nation that "victory has a hundred fathers, but defeat is an orphan." He concluded, "I am the responsible officer of the government." Kennedy's admission, which differed from more halfhearted apologies by other presidents, engendered trust and caused his popularity to rise, enabling him to execute policies reevaluating the Cold War ethos and leading to a nuclear test–ban treaty.[66]

— *v* —

Accountability goes far beyond executive transparency and integrity. When I speak publicly, CEOs often ask how they can make their people more accountable to the organization. I tell them there's no such thing. People must be accountable to themselves, not to an organization. If we cannot keep promises we make to ourselves, like losing weight and getting more exercise—things that ultimately meet our normal human needs—then how can we keep promises to benefit others?

> At the end of the day, "organizational accountability" is nothing more than the sum of all individuals' accountability to their promises and to the ideal outcomes that will meet everyone's need.
>
> —Ron Karr

Accountability is most often seen in those who value their own word as well as that of others. For this reason, it is a trait to be looked for in the hiring process, and one that new hires look for when they join an organization. They need to trust what others say—and do—in relationship to their common goal.

In chapter 7, I recounted Kennedy's audacious goal of landing a man on the moon. How NASA executed on that strategy has been broken down into four significant disciplines,[67] the first of which is "Focus on the Wildly Important." Finding that all-important, all-consuming objective is the essence of the "clean piece of paper" exercise in chapter 6. Once you have everyone's buy-in to that ideal objective, the formula for successful execution is to hold everyone (including yourself) accountable for the steps leading to that goal. Don't focus on lagging indicators, like poor sales results or missing profitability goals. Instead, focus on leading indicators, the milestones you have identified that are critical to the outcome you etched on that "clean piece of paper" that will get you there. If you are not meeting these milestones, ask questions: "What can we do differently?" and "What will make the difference in reaching our destination?"

Contrast this strategy with the way many executives and their companies fail to execute change successfully. After the introduction of the Apple iPhone, Microsoft chairman Bill Gates tasked his then CEO, Steve Ballmer, with the job of creating a copycat device.[68] Despite a six-figure R&D budget, the project was a spectacular failure. Part of the problem was the company's performance evaluation system, which pitted employees against each other and encouraged teams to self-focus and self-isolate, for fear of being out-performed by others. They did not share a common vision, nor did they trust that others would pursue that vision and not their own self-interest.

Simply copying others' actions merely to make more money or earn status created drag and resistance, not velocity.

The process of mutual accountability starts with having the end in sight—one that everyone can align with—and then working backward to identify key, measurable milestones toward that end, as well as roadblocks that would rob you of that velocity. These milestones are your leading indicators, the wins needed in order to encourage everyone in the tasks of executing a strategy.

— *v* —

Finally, the third leadership quality needed to effectively execute a velocity strategy is inspiration or, more specifically, the practice of *celebration*. By giving team members occasion to celebrate meeting specific milestones (leading indicators), you create the right conditions for maximum velocity.

This has nothing to do with a leader's personal charisma or with having a "feel-good" event for its own sake. Entertaining the troops is not a bad thing, but unless a celebration is tied to genuine accomplishment, it will not affect the group's long-term capacity to align their actions with an ideal outcome.

As a sales/leadership coach, I have advocated two types of celebration, both of which are essential to executing a successful velocity strategy. The first is *individual* celebration, without which a leader will have difficulty inspiring others. Recently, in the disruptive times after the COVID-19 outbreak, I have met with executives who, in their haste to cope with the immediate crisis, fail to celebrate their own milestones. I asked one client who was focused on the negative if his small company had made their numbers for the quarter. They had done so, so I told him how important it was to celebrate *that*.

The stress of reinventing his business, amplified by the pandemic, was real. He lost sight of how far he was ahead of the game compared to most business owners dealing with COVID-19 He needed to feel, appreciate, and celebrate his accomplishment and what *had* been achieved in order to preserve his physical and emotional equilibrium.

As I noted in chapter 8, the act of completing a task successfully and consciously recognizing that completion triggers a positive emotional response. The act of celebration can be as simple as checking off a completed task. As Scott Halford noted, anxiety can result not only from stress or danger but also from incomplete tasks.[69] So the simple celebration of completing a milestone is a step toward attaining our own personal velocity. It will help us counter our own limiting thoughts and lead others in achieving the desired outcome.

The second type of celebration is *organizational*. When team members are regularly and publicly acknowledged for significant achievements, not only does morale go up but also overall team performance is significantly improved.

Celebrating meaningful efforts and achievements satisfies our psychological need for inclusion, appreciation, collaboration, and basic human contact. Practiced regularly, it greatly enhances creativity and confidence to take greater initiative. According to research at the University of Cambridge[70] and elsewhere, celebration conversations result in elevated levels of oxytocin, which enhances our willingness to take risks and handle challenges. They also release dopamine, which increases our ability to pay attention to critical tasks and ignore distracting information. The same studies indicate a significant lowering of cortisol levels, diminishing the likelihood of a fight-or-flight response and encouraging a more calm, thoughtful response.

I have seen the results of organizational celebration many times.

In 2016, G. J. Hart, the CEO of California Pizza Kitchen (CPK), hosted a meeting of my CRO mastermind group at his headquarters in Playa Vista, California. CPK, with over three hundred restaurants and fourteen thousand employees around the world, was in the midst of a successful financial turnaround. During our meeting, G. J. invited me to witness an exceptional example of organizational celebration.

Every quarter, CPK holds a ceremony honoring the recipient of the company's "ROCK Award." The acronym stands for the company's core philosophy—Respect, Opportunity, Communication, and Kindness—and the award is given to a team member whose application of that philosophy contributed to CPK's success. Interestingly, the award recipient is chosen by the previous quarter's winner, and the achievement is prominently memorialized with a plaque on a gigantic rock at CPK headquarters, where the ceremony takes place.

The event itself was memorable. The recipient, a junior network administrator, was acknowledged for his accomplishments, work ethic, and character by his boss and coworkers. The ceremony included gifts representing his passions (whiskey and garlic) and recorded video remarks from his fiancée, who could not leave work for the occasion. His parents were also invited to attend, and they shared stories of their son. They were beaming—as was he. Imagine being celebrated like this for your work results, with the entire HQ staff taking time out of their day to join the celebration. CPK had discovered that when that recognition is celebrated by the entire staff, it generates an energy that radiates out to the restaurants and positively impacts customer experiences, which in turn has resulted in significant sales growth.

I have encouraged other firms to do likewise, holding celebratory dinners or similar events upon successful completion of a milestone or goal. Without exception, CEOs have recounted the extraordinary emotional impact of singling out individuals for their contributions—an impact that has figured prominently in their companies' ongoing success.

Celebration and praise must be well-deserved and sincere. When it is, team members have a factual basis for the good feelings they experience. In the words of Benchmark Communications CEO Judith Glaser, such employees will "take more risks, speak up more, push back when they have things to say, and be more confident in their dealings with their peers."[71] When it comes to moving forward and executing a strategy, such motivated team members are indispensable.

— *v* —

When I coach leaders, no matter how successful they have been in the past, I often find that they suffer from the same things that plague all of us. They include self-doubt, feelings of fraud, uncertainty about taking risks, and the many other barriers mentioned throughout this book.

What separates them from the rest of us is that they have been captured by that "Thought in Formless Substance," an idea for which they don't have all the answers but toward which they will bend every conceivable resource. They are that one person out of twenty who drove by a dilapidated building and chose *not* to ignore the possible outcome, despite the risk of failure. They are comfortable with not having all the answers up front, and so continue to ask the right questions and hire or partner with the right people needed to execute that singular idea.

It's not always an easy road. Sometimes they fall victim to a paradox, as we all do. When consulting executives, I can find myself asking, "Why am I still having the same conversation with this person on the same issue as last year? They're smart, but they haven't moved the needle, which has impacted their ability to lead." The answer is, *they are stopped by their own roadblocks*. Their old thinking—limiting thoughts and past experiences, as discussed in chapter 2—is no longer relevant. But it has prevented them from achieving their ideal outcome, no matter how successful they may have been in the past. They are not realizing their true potential.

Changing this doesn't happen overnight. You can hear the same concept ten times without it impacting you, but the eleventh time, it blows you away—as if hearing it for the first time. It happens because you are different, the times are different, and the situation is different. It happens when instead of dealing with symptoms of resistance, you start dealing with the root cause—your old way of thinking. When this happens, they can achieve true velocity.

Whenever old thinking and limiting thoughts impede velocity, it is never our job to "change people." It is to help them see (and feel) the things that are stopping them and help them to come up with ways to do things differently. Personal development, the removal of obstacles in oneself, is as great a factor in successful execution as is the presence or absence of resources—probably greater. Whenever you are faced with the paradox of drag and resistance (and it will happen a lot), the question should not be, "Why did this go wrong?" but "What could I have done differently?"

The secret to moving forward is not to focus on what went wrong or what we don't want or like in a given situation. Those responses are purely defensive, noncreative, and limiting. The secret is to focus on *objectives*: solutions that are meant not simply to make money but to fulfill a greater need. Such actions foster willingness, creativity, and openness to any possibility.

Having the right mindset is important, but that will not matter unless we *do* something with it. By that I mean doing the tasks that actually support an ideal outcome, rather than doing things to no purpose. As a Japanese proverb puts it, "Vision without action is a daydream. Action without vision is a nightmare."

The intent of this book is not to merely state the principles of a velocity mindset but to enable you to put them into practice, both personally and professionally—the hallmark of true leadership.

13 COMMUNICATION, THE HEART OF LEADERSHIP

EXPERTS SINCE CHARLES DARWIN'S DAY HAVE disagreed on when humans developed the power of speech. Estimates vary widely between two million and fifty thousand years ago.[72] But whenever it happened, we began turning thoughts into sounds that could be heard and understood by others. It was a brilliant milestone for our species, but it also created a problem that leaders must cope with to this day.

Animal sounds can't be faked; a cat is incapable of purring ironically. But human speech is different. When we communicate, we assign *meaning* to our sounds and symbols. That meaning may be clear and even truthful to the one sending the message but not necessarily to the one receiving it. We *encode* our messages, but if the recipient *decodes* them incorrectly and doesn't give the sender the necessary feedback, the communication is ineffective.

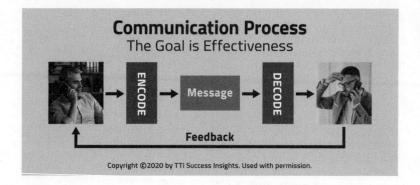

It's all about emotional connection. As we discussed in chapter 3, *a leader is responsible for creating the right psychological environment that is conducive to conversation*—being aware of the cortisol responses of others and finding ways to communicate that do not trigger others in unproductive ways. When the sender encodes a message, he does so according to his own biases and experiences. Likewise, the receiver decodes the messages according to *her* biases and experiences. This is where a breakdown in communication happens, when the sender does not consider the mindset and assumptions of the recipient. Just because a sender transmitted word sounds or written symbols does *not* mean they communicated. Communication is successful only when the message "lands" with the same intent with which it was sent.

Why is this so important? Throughout history, any business success or failure can be traced to this particular skill—the ability to communicate effectively with an audience. There are companies with good products and services who fail miserably. There are also companies whose products or services seemed strange or untenable, like Facebook, PayPal, or the Pet Rock, and yet succeeded beyond anyone's wildest dreams. The secret was effective communication.

There are two aspects of our nature in play when it comes to communication:

The Mind—That part of us that determines how a particular task or goal is to be accomplished.

The Heart—This is the essential *what* in the process, the actual goal or aspiration that matters—to both the sender and the recipient. This is where actual, emotional connection takes place.

Communication breaks down when the sender is focused on the *how* with no regard for *what* is important to the recipient. It's what happens when a salesperson launches into a discussion of features without taking any interest in the prospect's needs or challenges. It's what happens when a manager focuses on a procedural matter— large or small—without bothering to know what matters in the larger scheme of things. In chapter 8, the supervisor upset with an employee's excessive cell phone use failed to communicate because he focused on the *symptom* of unacceptable work delays. But when he pivoted and linked the conversation to the employee's desire to become a master welder (a *what* that benefited everyone), his communication was successful.

To have this kind of communication, you must have a rapport with the person or persons involved. The word "rapport" does not mean creating favorable social relationships, like having dinner or drinks with a client, as salespeople were often urged to do in the 1980s. Rather, rapport involves a relationship built on the leader's willingness to help others achieve *their* desired outcomes. It has to do with others' wants, motivations, and basic needs. As we'll see later in the chapter, it requires the appropriate level of empathy, without sacrificing your own core objectives and those of your organization. However, in order to lead your team to its greatest potential velocity, communication based in the heart is essential.

— *v* —

Most leaders have difficulty when it comes to having *the tough conversations*, otherwise known as the big elephant in the room. These happen when, even though you understand the other person's needs and have some level of rapport, there are still problems with no good solution. They can involve things like telling a customer you won't be able to meet a deadline or telling a team member that their performance is unsatisfactory, that their idea won't work, or the ultimate bad news that they have to be let go. This difficulty is understandable. Most leaders are decent human beings who don't want to hurt others. (Personally, I prefer to work with such people; their reluctance is a sign they are human and care about others.) But when they overagonize about conversations affecting others' futures, it can lead to procrastination. When that happens, it only delays the inevitable conversation and reduces velocity—both their own velocity as a leader as well as that of the team member, partner, or customer.

The longer we avoid a tough conversation—one that's causing us grief, tension, or lack of fulfillment—the more that resistance will rob us of velocity. So it's incumbent on a leader to have those conversations as soon as possible by communicating effectively and in the context of ideal outcomes.

The first step, of course, is to understand the whole situation—not just the symptoms or how the issue affects you in the moment. You need to assess the impacts on the person involved, and on the group or organization as a whole. To get past the natural reluctance over possibly hurting someone, you need to adopt the mindset that you're trying to help them. This is difficult, but you need to realize that, in most cases, behavior that is reducing your organization's velocity is likely doing the same for the person themselves.

The best way to start that conversation is to have the person talk about the frustrations they are having. Besides giving you a clearer picture of their needs and objectives, that will also give you an opening to discuss your frustrations and ask if they have any possible solutions.

Here's an example of a tough conversation and how it turned to a positive outcome. At the time of my mother's accident, as I related in chapter 8, I was already in a difficult position regarding my own job. It was in the mid-1980s; the tech industry was undergoing upheavals over the rise of personal computers. But my unglamorous job was northeast territory manager for a communication board manufacturer. I was successful sales-wise, but my role, involving calling on engineers, repeatedly, to dig up leads, was unsatisfying and demotivating, to say the least. Don't get me wrong. These were, and still are, great people. But delving into the bits and bytes of the matter was just not my cup of tea.

When the accident occurred and for the following month, I diverted all my attention to dealing with effects of the accident. As the emergency became less critical and I had time to breathe, I came to realize *life is too short.* I had been constantly on a rapid treadmill, running to keep up with the tasks at hand and not paying attention to the true destiny I wanted to create for myself. So, when I returned, I had to have a difficult conversation with my executive VP about my situation. He knew and empathized with my personal situation, but we agreed that there were limited options: a change in my position, a change in the product set, or the need for me to move on. The first two were not possible, but he asked a significant question: "What do you want to do?" I said I had thought about starting a sales training practice based on my success in the field. Remarkably, his openness to that idea and his guidance in developing a business plan led me in 1988 to the successful launch of my career as a sales/leadership coach.

Because of the emotional connection stemming from that conversation, I learned a fundamental truth. Effective communication must include honesty, a genuine care and concern for the person you're communicating with, and putting the heart foremost—discovering *what* the goals and aspirations of that person are. Creating that emotional connection, meeting emotional needs instead of merely transactional ones, gives the other person a reason to engage in the conversation. Even if their goals don't coincide with yours, the communication will be effective.

— *v* —

Another important aspect of communication involves the *alignment of values*. Rather than trying to change people or overwhelm them with what you feel is important (self-focus), a real conversation always involves discovering the value system of the other person. If their values are compatible with yours, always base the discussion on that foundation.

One of the key concepts I taught as a sales coach was to get the blessing and support of the prospect's *key executives*. This is no small task. High-level executives are not interested in hearing about products and services; they have people for that. But when you connect on the basis of values, that is a different story.

One of my clients and friends, the president of a construction equipment leasing company, had an opportunity to call on the CEO of a Fortune 100 company that was a logical potential prospect. During their hour-long conversation, not a single word of my friend's company or services was mentioned. Instead, he told me, they spent the hour talking about McDonald's. When I expressed surprise, he explained that the CEO was an admirer of the fast-food chain's *flexibility* in customizing menu offerings to countries that, for example, did not hold with eating pork. The conversation was not really about fast food. The CEO was interested in my friend's company's values, namely flexibility. Flexibility was the key to that prospect's global strategy, and they wanted to ensure that all their partners have the same values. Because they communicated on that level and discovered a mutual alignment of values, my friend was recommended to those responsible for procuring construction equipment.

Values are issues of the heart. Together with human wants, needs, and the basic desire to eliminate pain or gain pleasure, they are the basis for emotional connection. They encompass *what* is important—to another individual and, by extension, to the group of people that comprise a company or organization. You cannot change someone's values, any more than you can change them as people. When executives try to change behavior—the *how* part of the equation—they inevitably fail. No one wants to be "fixed." But when they find alignment with the other's values, the communication becomes significantly more meaningful and effective.

Communication must also be *in context*. People make decisions for their own reasons, not yours. They will always translate (decode) what you say according to their own wants, biases, and experiences. So it is always important to frame the conversation in the context of what matters to the other person. Whenever you do so, it is an acknowledgment that you understand who that person is—that you heard them. It satisfies a fundamental need, regardless of whether or not your objectives are the same.

One challenge for sales executives or anyone trying to influence others is basing a conversation on what they believe the other person needs. Often, they do not gain buy-in. Why? There is no emotional connection yet. In sales, we say sell them what they "want" (emotional outcomes) and then give them what they need. Be careful how you read that statement, however. This is not about manipulating others. If you think it is, then you are not in the leadership Velocity Mindset®. This is about gaining someone's full attention, which will then allow you to enter a conversation that you know will serve the other person well.

The context of communication differs from one person to another. An employee will have a different set of desires and expectations than a shareholder or a client. But the fundamental need for connection, recognition, and value is the same. Once that emotional connection is made, then meaningful communication is possible.

When a leader is seeking a common outcome for the entire team, a common mistake is to communicate it the same way to all team members. This will not gain universal buy-in. You need to *customize the message* to the wants and motivations of each individual, or you will wind up with a team that is not pulling in the same direction or with the same velocity.

A good example of message customization is former New York Giants coach Bill Parcells, whose team won two Super Bowls in 1987 and 1991. Parcells had two leaders and stars on his team: Hall of Fame linebacker Lawrence Taylor and star quarterback Phil Simms. In his role as "master psychologist," Parcells communicated with the two players very differently, based on the differences in the players' makeup and the type of relationship he had with each.[73] They were all going for the same objective, a Super Bowl win. But he pushed and motivated each one differently, because they each had different emotions and triggers. As the old saying goes, "different strokes for different folks." It is not that people should be treated differently in terms of fairness. It is about communicating in a way that will move each person forward.

— *v* —

The final aspect of a leader's capacity to communicate is *empathy*. Simply stated, this is our ability "to recognize, understand, and share the thoughts and feelings of another . . ."[74] It is not the same as sympathy, which is a feeling of sorrow for someone else's misfortune.[75] Empathy can be cognitive (*knowing* what another person may be thinking or feeling), emotional (actually *feeling* what he or she is feeling), or compassionate (moved to act on their behalf). It is an essential part of successful communication because it takes the leader out of their own biases and experience and gives them a more accurate view of the other's needs and aspirations.

Of course, there is such a thing as too much empathy. When communicating with a team member or a potential prospect, identifying *completely* with another's priorities can result in abandoning your own. It can also result in your mirroring and amplifying their stress, anxiety, and anger, unleashing a cortisol reaction[76] that can lead to feelings of helplessness or depression.

But in good measure, empathy is the ideal ingredient of good communication. It informs the listener that he or she is being heard and that their wants and needs are legitimate. It counters the potential cortisol reaction to an otherwise tough conversation. It also allows the leader to acknowledge a difficult situation without accepting blame for it. Most of all, it provides the emotional connection and the opportunity to PAUSE and discuss mutually beneficial outcomes and aspirations.

Always remember, if you are not empathetic, you will not be asking the right questions, if any. You will probably be working under your own assumptions, which very often will not reflect the reality of the situation. It will leave you wondering why you did not gain velocity in your ability to influence others.

— *v* —

Without question, communication is a soft skill, one that requires intuition, practice, and patience. Although I have listed some of the main requirements, it cannot be done by rote or by following a checklist. But in the end, good communication is the basis for aligning members of a team, a sales relationship, or a partnership with the leader's vision for a desirable outcome. It is the final step in attaining velocity.

Remember this golden rule: people buy in for their own individual reasons, not yours!

CONCLUSION
WHAT DOES IT ALL MEAN?

MY PURPOSE IN WRITING THIS BOOK is not to dictate or control how you conduct your life or your business dealings. I can say without a shadow of doubt that *I do not know it all*. (My colleagues and close friends will heartily agree with this assessment, for which I am grateful.) I have made enough mistakes in life to know that I could have achieved much more, had I embraced these principles sooner. So the purpose of this book is to help others who, like myself, want more out of life.

As one gets older and presumably wiser, it's a natural tendency to share one's experiences to help others avoid similar mistakes and gain velocity in their lives. We see this with our kids. My daughter is an amazing and accomplished young professional. And yet, like many parents, I see things in her reminiscent of my earlier days—things that did not serve me well. As you can imagine, sharing those concerns often elicits the response, "I know what I'm doing." Sure enough, in their own way, our kids make similar mistakes as we did and learn from them.

Maybe people have to go through the various stages of growth to gain experience—that is, unless they receive counsel from those who have gone before. I think it is a combination of both.

Just as I was finishing this book and about to complete the hand-off to my publisher, I received a fresh opportunity to exercise these principles in my own life. As I recounted in the introduction, I was faced with the prospect of open-heart surgery. Once again, I had the opportunity to PAUSE, visualize the ideal outcome, and recognize my own limiting thoughts, past experience, and brain chemistry. I needed to have the tough conversations—and *listen* to the answers.

This latest exercise in velocity had an unexpected bonus. My incomparable surgeon literally checked every box and demonstrated all the qualities of leadership described in this book. She was empathetic, listened openly, was willing to have the tough conversations, and always proceeded with the end in sight.

As I recounted in the introduction, the surgery was a success in more ways than one. The physical defect in my heart was skillfully repaired, and I am on the path to full recovery. More importantly, I have yet another reminder of the *power* of having a Velocity Mindset®.

— *v* —

There are two ways of building a life, a career, or a business. One is organically, by making the same mistakes others have made and learning from them. The other is the Velocity Mindset® way: by learning from others' mistakes as well as your own and avoiding unnecessary failures. In business we refer to this as acquisition. You can build a business from scratch, or you can acquire other businesses and reach your desired market share and profitability by leveraging the success of others.

The choice is yours. The key is to come to terms with your own self-induced obstacles that create drag and resistance to your velocity. For so long as your own velocity is affected, it will cascade downward, negatively impacting the velocity of those who count on you.

Not all businesses and life experiences are alike. Not every detail in this book will apply to your personal or professional life. But I am suggesting that you take an honest assessment of where you are headed, where you want to be headed, and ensure your tasks and mindset are supportive of your goals. Otherwise, you will be working hard without the fulfillment you desire. So see what resonates with you, and use these principles to fill in your own gaps.

Whatever you do, remember that personal velocity is the key to professional velocity.

It's simple. Whether you have an official title or not, you can become a better leader, over the things in your personal life, your professional life, or both. (Actually, it works both ways. Those who exercise good leadership qualities in personal matters tend to do the same in business, and vice versa.) Velocity—speed, direction, and alignment—is the secret.

From the stories and examples and from the many principles I've learned along the way, I have aspired to create a roadmap of sorts. This book presents not only the *how* aspects of leadership but also a picture of *what* true leadership entails. It's not enough to have a series of memorized steps if you don't know where you're going.

After reading this book, I hope you'll take the time to PAUSE and recalibrate. Consider the things that are important to your organization and your life—in other words, your ideal outcome. Start with a clean piece of paper, literally, and don't assume you have or need to have all the answers up front. Like I said, it's all about the art of the PAUSE, slowing down long enough to visualize your destination. Once you have that end result in mind, ask yourself if you've set up the tasks and milestones to get you there. They don't need to be perfect. Trust me; you will get things wrong. But as long as you make failure an opportunity to learn, you will achieve velocity.

Equally important, ask if you have the right people with you to help reach that ideal outcome. No one can do it alone. You're looking for a combination of competence and alignment of purpose. Don't look for people who provide sympathy; look for empathy in your team members, but especially in yourself.

I can assure you there will be barriers, not only in events and people you encounter, but also in yourself. The hardest thing I'll ask you to do is to constantly monitor the emotional roadblocks you create for yourself. These can be negative thoughts, fears, assumptions, procrastination, perfectionism—anything that stops you from executing your velocity strategy. Once again, let me reiterate, when you PAUSE and identify these limiting thoughts and habits for what they are and keep your ideal outcome in mind, you will be able to regain velocity. (Spoiler alert: When you learn to trust your intuition, you'll find this becomes easier.)

As I've learned from experience, it's easy to allow past suffering and disappointment cloud our judgment, keep us from exercising our creative instincts, and obscure what was once a clear and compelling vision. It does not need to be so. There are no guarantees, and I'm not talking about "fluff" or wishful thinking. But I am convinced it is up to each of us to create our own destiny, to start with the end in mind, and take the steps needed to get there.

— *v* —

Do not get discouraged. Many people attempt to envision their ideal destiny but still end up with the results of the past. Why? Because they allow past experiences and limiting thoughts to cloud their judgment of what's truly possible. Their vision and actions are limited by their biases and experiences. To grow, we cannot allow these to be the controlling factors. Instead, our past experiences should be combined with our intuition to help prevent us from making unnecessary mistakes. We will still make mistakes, of course, and we should get used to them. It's all a part of growth.

When you identify your ideal destiny, remember that the actions and tasks you used in the past will *not* be strong enough to get you to the finish line of that new, desired outcome. If they were strong enough to do so, then you would have already achieved that outcome. The trick is to see, unemotionally, what traits from the past you should enhance and which ones you should discard in order to reach your new destination.

And as you pursue your ideal outcome, don't be surprised when s**t happens or, as a less vulgar, more profound, Yiddish proverb puts it, "Man plans, and God laughs." Our velocity strategy may be sound, but when and if plans are upended (they will be), then the true test of a leader is what they do next. Can they laugh, listen, keep the end in sight, have empathy, and keep making intuitive decisions?

— *v* —

As we move through the various stages of life, after we have reached our current level of success, there comes a point in time when we start asking ourselves, "What did it all mean? Where is the significance in my life?"

Like most people, I like to attain the finer things. But no matter how much money you make, that feeling of accomplishment pales in comparison to the feeling of knowing you have helped someone else move forward in life. When I lose a deal or experience similar setbacks, I can be having a miserable day. But that depleted feeling has often been replaced instantaneously with a feeling of fulfillment when I receive a simple call from someone thanking me for something I wrote or said that made a tremendous difference in their lives.

I hope you have found a renewed energy from reading this book on how you can lead your own life with more purpose and be a leader in life that helps others find fulfillment and significance. You can only do this when you keep your eye on the destination you are truly after and not get sidetracked with emotions, fears, and limiting thoughts that remove you from the game you should be playing.

If you genuinely want to live with a Velocity Mindset® and live life to the fullest, you must remember:

Velocity = Speed with Direction

Without direction, you only achieve burnout and fall short of your desired outcomes. I hope this book has made you think about what's important, what steps are next, and with whom you plan to take them. Together, you can become leaders in a new Velocity Mindset®.

ENDNOTES

1   M. Scott Peck, *The Road Less Travelled* (New York: Simon & Schuster, 1978).

2   Ibid.

3   "Velocity," Britannica.com (*Encyclopedia Britannica,* 2020), www.britannica.com/science/velocity.

4   John E. Sarno, *Healing Back Pain: The Mind-Body Connection* (New York: Warner Books, 1991).

5   Kimberly Fries, "8 Essential Qualities That Define Great Leadership," *Forbes,* Forbes Media LLC, May 23, 2018, www.forbes.com/sites/kimberlyfries/2018/02/08/8-essential-qualities-that-define-great-leadership.

6   "Understanding the Differences: Leadership vs. Management," *go2HR*, go2 Tourism HR Society, 2020, www.go2hr.ca/retention-engagement/understanding-the-differences-leadership-vs-management.

7   Nancy K. Napier, PhD, "The Myth of Multitasking," *Psychology Today*, Sussex Publishers, May 12, 2014, www.psychologytoday.com/us/blog/creativity-without-borders/201405/the-myth-multitasking.

8   Ibid.

9   Sophie McLean, *The Elegance of Simplicity: A Wisdom Teacher's Epic Journey to Awareness* (self-published).

10   Michèle Shuster, *Biology for a Changing World, With Physiology*, Second Edition, (New York: W. H. Freeman, Macmillan Learning, 2018).

11 "Cortisol," *You and Your Hormones*, Society for Endocrinology, January 2019, www.yourhormones.info/hormones/cortisol/.

12 Lindsey Konkel, "Cortisol: Everything You Need to Know About the 'Stress Hormone,'" *Everyday Health*, September 6, 2018, https://www.everydayhealth.com/cortisol/guide/.

13 Scott G. Halford, *Activate Your Brain: How Understanding Your Brain Can Improve Your Work—and Your Life* (Austin, Texas: Greenleaf Book Group Press, 2015).

14 Scott Halford, interview, July 8, 2020.

15 Jade Wu, "The Power of Oxytocin," *Psychology Today*, Sussex Publishers, February 11, 2020, https://www.psychologytoday.com/us/blog/the-savvy-psychologist/202002/the-power-oxytocin.

16 "Dopamine," *Psychology Today,* https://www.psychologytoday.com/us/basics/dopamine.

17 "Dopamine affects how brain decides whether a goal is worth the effort," *NIH Research Matters*, National Institutes of Health, March 31, 2020, https://www.nih.gov/news-events/nih-research-matters/dopamine-affects-how-brain-decides-whether-goal-worth-effort.

18 "Burnout," *Psychology Today*, https://www.psychologytoday.com/us/basics/burnout.

19 "Burnout," *Mind-Body-Health.ne*t, https://www.mind-body-health.net/burnout.shtml.

20 Barry Farber, *Crisis in Education: Stress and Burnout in the American Teacher* (San Francisco: Jossey-Bass).

21 Sharon Martin, LCSW, "Is It Fear of Failure or Fear of Success?" *PsychCentral*, Psych Central Community Connection Inc., October 25, 2019, https://blogs.psychcentral.com/imperfect/2016/01/is-it-fear-of-failure-or-fear-of-success/.

22 "List of Major League Baseball Career Batting Average Leaders," Wikipedia, https://en.wikipedia.org/wiki/List_of_Major_League_Baseball_career_batting_average_leaders.

23 Theo Tsaousides, "Why Fear of Failure Can Keep You Stuck," *Psychology Today*, Sussex Publishers, December 20, 2017, www.psychologytoday.com/us/blog/smashing-the-brain-blocks/201712/why-fear-failure-can-keep-you-stuck.

24 John E. Sarno, *Healing Back Pain: The Mind-Body Connection* (New York: Warner Books, 1991).

25 Ibid.

26 John E. Sarno, *The Mindbody Prescription: Healing the Body, Healing the Pain* (New York: Warner Books, 1998).

27 Ibid., p. 22.

28 Susanne Babbel, PhD, "Fear of Success," *Psychology Today*, Sussex Publishers, January 3, 2003, https://www.psychologytoday.com/us/blog/somatic-psychology/201101/fear-success.

29 Jenika McDavitt, "Fear of Success: Do You Have One Of These 6 Symptoms?" *Psychology for Photographers (and Other Creative Professionals)*, Jenika McDavitt LLC, March 2, 2016, https://psychologyforphotographers.com/fear-of-success-symptoms.

30 Stephen Shapiro, *Invisible Solutions: 25 Lenses that Reframe and Help Solve Difficult Business Problems* (Herndon, VA: Amplify Publishing, 2020).

31 "What is Lean?" Lean Enterprise Institute, www.lean.org/WhatsLean.

32 James P. Womack, *Gemba Walks* (Cambridge, MA: Lean Enterprise Institute, 2011).

33 Alan Spoon, "What 'Pivot' Really Means," *Inc.*, Mansueto Ventures, August 10, 2012, www.inc.com/alan-spoon/what-pivot-really-means.html.

34 Srinivasan Pillay, MD, "The Science of Visualization: Maximizing Your Brain's Potential During the Recession," *The Huffington Post*, April 3, 2009, https://www.huffpost.com/entry/the-science-of-visualizat_b_171340.

35 Robert X. Cringely, *Accidental Empires: How the Boys of Silicon Valley Make Their Millions, Battle Foreign Competition, and Still Can't Get a Date*, (Boston: Addison-Wesley Publishing Co., 1992).

36 Sean Braswell, "The Agreement That Catapulted Microsoft Over IBM," *OZY*, May 29, 2019, https://www.ozy.com/true-and-stories/the-agreement-that-catapulted-microsoft-over-ibm/94437/.

37 "Steve Jobs iPhone 2007 Presentation," Macworld Expo, January 9, 2007, https://www.youtube.com/watch?v=vN4U5FqrOdQ.

38 *John F. Kennedy Moon Speech—Rice Stadium*, September 12, 1962, https://er.jsc.nasa.gov/seh/ricetalk.htm.

39 Academy of Program/Project & Engineering Leadership, *Dr. Henry Pohl on the Keys to Apollo's Success, APPEL Knowledge Services*, February 27, 2010, https://appel.nasa.gov/2010/02/27/ao_2-1_f_pohl-html/.

40 Wallace Wattles, *The Science of Getting Rich* (London: Penguin Books, 2007).

41 Ibid.

42 Ibid.

43 Ibid.

44 Lewis Carroll and Martin Gardner, Editor, *The Annotated Alice* (New York: Clarkson N. Potter, Inc./Publisher, 1960).

45 Scott G. Halford, *Activate Your Brain: How Understanding Your Brain Can Improve Your Work—and Your Life* (Austin, Texas: Greenleaf Book Group Press, 2015).

46 Scott G. Halford, "5 Simple Ways to Retrain Your Brain," *Credit Union National Association News,* May 25, 2017, https://news.cuna.org/articles/112347-simple-ways-to-retrain-your-brain.

47 Lauren Suval, Stress and the Concept of Control, *PsychCentral,* Psych Central Community Connection Inc., July 8, 2018, https://psychcentral.com/blog/stress-and-the-concept-of-control/.

48 Competitive Edge Inc. website, www.competitiveedgeinc.com/about-us/judy-suiter/.

49 "Intuition," *Psychology Today*, https://www.psychologytoday.com/intl/basics/intuition.

50 Daniel Kahneman, *Thinking, Fast and Slow* (New York: Farrar, Straus and Giroux, 2011).

51 Ron Karr and Don Blohowiak, *The Complete Idiot's Guide to Great Customer Service* (Indianapolis: Alpha Books/Penguin Group, 1997).

52 Claudia Hammond, "When Should You Follow Your Gut Instinct?" *BBC Future*, November 5, 2019, https://www.bbc.com/future/article/20191031-when-should-you-follow-your-gut-instinct.

53 Suzanne Degges-White, PhD, "Dealing with Zoom Anxiety," *Psychology Today*, April 13, 2020, https://www.psychologytoday.com/us/blog/lifetime-connections/202004/dealing-zoom-anxiety.

54 "Financial Leverage," *BusinessDictionary,* ZDNet / CBS Interactive, September 27, 2020, http://www.businessdictionary.com/definition/financial-leverage.html.

55 "Leverage," ibid., http://www.businessdictionary.com/definition/leverage.html.

56 Derek Muller, "The Science of Six Degrees of Separation," Veritasium, YouTube, August 25, 2015, https://www.youtube.com/watch?v=TcxZSmzPw8k&feature=youtu.be.

57 Vistage website, https://www.vistage.com.

58 YPO website, https://www.ypo.org/.

59 Boris Ewenstein et al., "Changing Change Management," *McKinsey Insights*, July 1, 2015, https://www.mckinsey.com/featured-insights/leadership/changing-change-management.

60 "Three Reasons Why Good Strategies Fail: Execution, Execution. . .", *Knowledge@Wharton*, Wharton School of Business, August 10, 2005, https://knowledge.wharton.upenn.edu/article/three-reasons-why-good-strategies-fail-execution-execution/.

61 Larry Bossidy and Ram Charam, *Execution: The Discipline of Getting Things Done*, (New York: Crown Business/Random House, 2002).

62 Ibid.

63 Ibid.

64 John Hall, "How to Walk the Talk with Your Leadership Message," *Forbes,* Forbes Media LLC, September 1, 2019, https://www.forbes.com/sites/johnhall/2019/09/01/how-to-walk-the-talk-with-your-leadership-message.

65 Jerry Knight, "Tylenol's Maker Shows How to Respond to Crisis," *The Washington Post*, October 11, 1982, https://www.washingtonpost.com/archive/business/1982/10/11/tylenols-maker-shows-how-to-respond-to-crisis/bc8df898-3fcf-443f-bc2f-e6fbd639a5a3/.

66 David Greenberg, "The Goal: Admitting Failure without Being a Failure," *The New York Times*, January 14, 2007, https://www.nytimes.com/2007/01/14/weekinreview/14green.html.

67 Chris McChesney, Sean Covey, and Jim Huling, *The 4 Disciplines of Execution: Achieving Your Wildly Important Goals*, (New York: Free Press/Simon & Schuster, 2012).

68 Quy Huy, "Five Reasons Most Companies Fail at Strategy Execution," *INSTEAD Knowledge,* Wharton School of Business, January 4, 2016, https://knowledge.insead.edu/blog/insead-blog/five-reasons-most-companies-fail-at-strategy-execution-4441.

69 Scott Halford, "5 Simple Ways to Retrain Your Brain," *Credit Union National Association News*, May 25, 2017, https://news.cuna.org/articles/112347-simple-ways-to-retrain-your-brain.

70 Judith E. Glaser, "Celebration Time: A Cocktail Each Executive Should Know How to Mix," *Psychology Today*, December 28, 2015, https://www.psychologytoday.com/us/blog/conversational-intelligence/201512/celebration-time.

71 Ibid.

72 Barbara J. King, "When Did Human Speech Evolve?" Cosmos & Culture, National Public Radio, September 5, 2013, https://www.npr.org/sections/13.7/2013/09/05/219236801/when-did-human-speech-evolve.

73 Dave Anderson, "Coach of Giants Sees Beyond the X's and O's," *The New York Times,* November 20, 1990, https://www.nytimes.com/1990/11/20/sports/coach-of-giants-sees-beyond-the-x-s-and-o-s.html.

74 "Empathy," *Psychology Today*, https://www.psychologytoday.com/us/basics/empathy.

75 Tchiki Davis, PhD, "Sympathy vs. Empathy," *Psychology Today*, July 14, 2020, https://www.psychologytoday.com/us/blog/click-here-happiness/202007/sympathy-vs-empathy.

76 Agata Blaszczak-Boxe, "Too Much Emotional Intelligence Is a Bad Thing," *Scientific American Mind*, March 1, 2017, https://www.scientificamerican.com/article/too-much-emotional-intelligence-is-a-bad-thing/.